Ralph Branca and
the Meaning of Life

Ralph Branca and the Meaning of Life
Bob Mitchell

McFarland & Company, Inc., Publishers
Jefferson, North Carolina

ISBN (print) 978-1-4766-9832-8
ISBN (ebook) 978-1-4766-5779-0

LIBRARY OF CONGRESS CATALOGING DATA ARE AVAILABLE

Library of Congress Control Number 2025032792

© 2025 Bob Mitchell. All rights reserved

No part of this book may be reproduced or transmitted in any form or by any means, electronic or mechanical, including photocopying or recording, or by any information storage and retrieval system, without permission in writing from the publisher.

Front cover illustration by Susan Ellen Love

Printed in the United States of America

*McFarland & Company, Inc., Publishers
Box 611, Jefferson, North Carolina 28640
www.mcfarlandpub.com*

*Again, to Susan Ellen Love,
who gives Meaning to my Life.*

Table of Contents

Acknowledgments — ix
Prologue. Metaphor! — 1

Part One—Cause and Effects — 7
ONE. Spaldeen — 9
TWO. Bedroom — 18
THREE. Green Room — 28
FOUR. Echoing Green — 35

Part Two—Agony of Defeat — 45
FIVE. Two Impostors — 47
SIX. It's a Shame — 57
SEVEN. Fail Better — 65
EIGHT. Losers Valiant — 71
NINE. Hope Abandoned — 79
TEN. Ancient Wisdom — 84

Part Three—The Human Side — 87
ELEVEN. Everyman — 89
TWELVE. Big Noise — 94
THIRTEEN. Thirteen — 103
FOURTEEN. Two Faces — 110
FIFTEEN. Pagliaccio — 123
SIXTEEN. (Scape)goat — 126

Table of Contents

Part Four—Crimes and Punishments   131

SEVENTEEN. Ralph and Adam   133
EIGHTEEN. Ralph and Job   139
NINETEEN. Ralph and Oedipus   145
TWENTY. Ralph and Hester   151
TWENTY-ONE. Ralph and Rodion   158
TWENTY-TWO. Ralph and Josef   162
TWENTY-THREE. Ralph and Sisyphus   166

Epilogue. Jean-Jacques: The Final Word   171
Bibliography   175
Index   177

Acknowledgments

To paraphrase Yogi, I'd like to thank everyone who made this book necessary.

First, of course, a huge tip of the cap to the two protagonists in the greatest, most compelling drama in baseball history, Ralph Branca and Bobby Thomson, without whom this book would quite obviously never have been conceived or written. And to you both, posthumously, a very Happy 75th Anniversary of The Game!

My heartfelt thanks to my outstanding and talented (and dare I say visionary?) editor at McFarland, kindred spirit and fellow baseball fanatic Gary Mitchem, who believed in, and supported, me and my writing from the very start.

My gratitude to the four preeminent members of the PBAW (Pantheon of Baseball Aficionados and Writers) who contributed lovely blurbs for this book: Peter Golenbock, Tim Kurkjian, Marty Appel, and George Will.

I am also grateful to the people who have enriched the considerable part of me that is athlete and coach and baseball fan and writer: Ernie Fleishman, Lonnie Hanauer, Jon Plaut, Larry Silver, Jim Grosfeld, Ralph Dupee, Bob Bell, Myron Ruckstull, Harlow Parker, and Clarence Chaffee (my coaches); Sal Maglie, Larry Jansen, Willie Mays, Monte Irvin, Don Mueller, Whitey Lockman, Wes Westrum, Hoyt Wilhelm, Minnie Minoso, Ralph Kiner, Robin Roberts, Richie Ashburn, Roberto Clemente, Warren Spahn, Hank Aaron, Frank Robinson, Stan Musial, Ted Williams, Al Kaline, Mickey Mantle, Jackie Robinson, Gil Hodges, Roy Campanella, Pee Wee Reese, and Duke Snider (the ballplayers I most admired growing up); Al Gorfin, Larry Palitz, Peter Badanes, Jon Maksik, Bob Liss, and Nat Greenfield (summer camp friends who pushed me to excel); Jim Blumstein, Peter Hummer, Mike Groothuis, Neil Lebowitz, Ronnie Rothstein, and Steve Weinstock (high-school teammates who pushed me to excel); Jim Kramer, Pete Allen, John

Acknowledgments

Storey, John Trainor, Budge Upton, Randy Prozeller, Gar Noll, Skip Caine, and Doug Ernst (college teammates who pushed me to excel); and Frank Fleizach, Kenny Horn, Ken Samelson, David Frantz, Roger Freilich, Hal Crowther, Ned Davis, Mark Groothuis, Jim Mangan, Pete Haller, David DeVries, John Sexton, and Frank Ittleman, all devoted baseball aficionados and friends who have supported my writing.

A special thanks to Avraham Merav, Michael Feld, George Smith, Alan Brown, and the wonderful and caring physicians at Cedars-Sinai Medical Center in LA (cardiologists Dael Geft, Jig Patel, Michelle Kittleson, Dave Chang, Jon Kobashigawa, Mike Shehata, and Michele Hamilton; and my life-saving cardiothoracic surgeon, Alfredo Trento), for keeping my heart beating, literally.

I'm especially grateful to the people who keep and have kept my heart beating, figuratively, with their unflagging love and friendship: my wonderful aunt Phyllis Clurman, stepdaughter Elissa Goodkin (and husband Dan and twins Lila and Emmy), sister-in-law Shelley London (and husband Phil), Lance and Mary Donaldson-Evans (and offspring Andrew and Catherine), the late and great Frank Fleizach, Hank and Elayne Gardstein, Kenny and Paula Horn, Tony Caprio and Dana Carton, the late and great Al Gorfin, Bob Liss, Mark Cripps, my adopted Finkelstein cousins (Lee and Evel, Ellen and Doug, Eric and Gail, and Steven and Nancy), Bill (sadly departed) and Beth Jaquith, David and Joanne Frantz, Leo and Margaret Schwartz, Pete and Linda Haller, Stan and Carroll Possick, Bob and Fran Rubin, Budge and Kyle Upton, Louie Neiheisel and Ann von Gal, Roger Freilich, Judith and Frédéric Bluysen, the late and great Seymon Ostilly and Hugh Herbert-Burns, Rony and Rachel Herz, Kip and Janet Pope, Bob and Kathi Roesler, Diane Cabaud (and daughters Nicole and Simone), Gil (sadly departed) and Barbara Feldman, Valerie Light and Bob Joseph, Ray and Gini La Charité, Robin Landa, Mike Appelbaum, Stu Seides, Howard and Karen Rogg, Marty Wasserman, David Lee Rubin, Jim and Judy Kramer, Pete Allen, Peter Bregman, Chuck (sadly departed) and Barbara DeBevoise, Suzanne Nash, Adriene Fern, Meredith Geisler, Carol Turturro, Alan Pearlman, Bailey Young, Jack Vroom, Gar Noll, Fred and Linda Thaler, Joel Drucker, Ken and Melinda Lindner, Kathy and Russ Doherty, Joe and Bev Gerber, Peter Gerstenfeld, John and Jane Gould, Bailey Young, Christa Granton, Ali Archer, Rich Stern, Herb Hochman, Alan Hoffman, Bob Shack, Robert Aberlin, Jack Florin, Jon Fratkin, Steve Green, Jim Blumstein, Si Trutt, Rich Spiegel, and Richard Jensen. And last but

Acknowledgments

not least, to my incredible, loving Italian friends Giuseppe Signorile and Maria Gravina (and sons Francesco and Filippo), Antonietta Cisterna and Francesco Scofano, Antonella Timpano and Marcello Olivari, Tania Calcinaro and Marco Croci, Susanna Trionfera, and Antonella Maione and Mauro Cazzaro: *Mille grazie per la vostra amicizia ed un fortissimo abbraccio a tutti voi!*

Sending lots of love, of course, to my amazing children: Noah (and Nina) Mitchell, Jenny (and Eric) Williams, and Sarah Mitchell (and John Demarest).

And most of all, to Susan Ellen Love, my incomparable wife and kindred spirit, Love of my life, accomplished artist, creative force, passionate soul, and indomitable warrior spirit.

Prologue
Metaphor!

Now it is done. Now the story ends. And there is no way to tell it. The art of fiction is dead. Reality has strangled invention. Only the utterly impossible, the inexpressibly fantastic, can ever be plausible again. —Red Smith

Deep down in the bowels of my soul, I cling to three profound, abiding convictions: 1. Passion and compassion are the keys to a meaningful existence; 2. Asparagus will never pass between my lips; and 3. Baseball is not just a sport—it is, at its very best, nothing less than a powerful metaphor for life itself.

Take, for example, the most famous, dramatic, and high-stakes event in the history of baseball in particular and American sports in general (in the opinion of not just me, but a stupendously large number of sportswriters, fans, aficionados, and experts): the October 3, 1951, third-and-deciding pennant playoff game between the Brooklyn Dodgers and their mortal enemies and Gotham rivals, the New York Giants. Bums and Jints. The Miracle at Coogan's Bluff. The Shot Heard 'Round the World. The Ralph Branca–Bobby Thomson ultimate showdown. The Comeback of All Times. The "The Giants Win the Pennant!" game.

The Game.

What transpired then as an epic battle, three-quarters of a century ago, has morphed into an epic, *period*, in the literary sense of an event that becomes expanded beyond its original impact and scope into a transcendent tale that will be recounted, in great and magnificent detail, to future generations until the last syllable of recorded time, as The Bard, via Macbeth, put it.

A better way to describe the epic significance of this one game is to employ the term *metaphor*, a figure of speech that equates something

Prologue

to a very different something else in a different realm, but both with a common quality (e.g., Shakespeare's "All the world's a stage," in *As You Like It*). Metaphors can convert complex ideas into powerful images that produce emotional reactions. So on Wednesday, 10/3/51, at precisely 3:58 p.m. Eastern time, there occurred the grand finale of a baseball game, yes, but this entire event has been transformed through the past many decades into more than an ordinary game by its metaphorical power.

For those living through it, it was, and still is, much more than just a competition contested on a field: it has become a vivid dream or nightmare, depending on for whom you were rooting. An intense and meaningful rite of passage, either way. And for many of those who were born or became sentient beings after that date, and who are real fans of baseball and enjoy watching and reading about its glorious history, this one game still represents, on a deep level, an entire gamut of paired conflicting human feelings and attributes, including courage and fear, hope and despair, pride and shame, success and failure, destiny and coincidence, fantasy and reality, effort and resignation, assets and flaws, absurdity and logic, and of course victory and defeat. Which is precisely what this book will attempt—as it peels back the metaphorical onion—to describe, ruminate upon, unravel, and articulate.

So why, of the well over 200,000 games—according to SABR—since the beginning of organized professional baseball in 1876, is *this one* so special, so impactful, so transcendent, so … metaphorical? To pilfer a line from Elizabeth Barrett Browning, let me count the ways:

1. *The Rivalry:* this contest was the only time that two teams in the same league in the same city—thus, particularly bitter rivals—competed in a postseason game (vs. Chicago, Boston, New York, and St. Louis, all of which cities were represented by teams in different leagues); 2. *The Hatred:* The rivalry between the Dodgers and the Giants was like no other in the history of the sport (the Yanks–Bosox and Cubs–Cards, for instance, run a distant second and third): the two teams hated each other—even more than I hate asparagus—to the point where Dodgers fans were said to have detested Halloween because its colors, black and orange, were the same as those of the odious Giants; 3. *The run-up to the game (part 1):* The Jints were thirteen-and-a-half games behind Dem Bums in August, then roared back to catch the Dodgers and force a pennant playoff, as all true baseball fans know; 4. *The run-up to the game (part 2):* They split the first two playoff games, of course, necessitating a

Prologue

winner-take-all Game 3; 5. *The run-up to the last inning:* Dodgers ahead, 4–1, going into the bottom of the ninth, etc., etc.; 6. *The run-up to Bobby Thomson's celebrated at-bat:* Dark singles, Mueller singles, Irvin fouls out, Lockman doubles, Mueller trashes his ankle (pinch runner: Clint Hartung), Bobby strides up to the dish with two on and one out and the Giants behind, now 4–2; 7. *The run-up to Branca coming in:* Newk getting visibly tired, Oisk throwing a curve down in the bullpen dirt, Sukeforth sends in Branca instead, etc., etc.

And the rest, as they say, is history. Or drama, rather. As in a Shakespearean tragedy, The Game reaches a crescendo, then a sudden, astounding, "utterly impossible" (to quote iconic sportswriter Red Smith) denouement—figuratively, the point at which the knot of all preceding elements is "untied," as will be, literally, the series itself. And in one fell swoop (the expression is, again, from Shakespeare's quill pen, this time from *Macbeth*), in one (in)famous pitch and one (in)famous swing of the bat, Bobby tomahawks Ralph's second pitch into the left-field stands in an improbable, unthinkable, instant climax to the instant baseball classic for the ages. And we have—instantly!—our baseball single-performance goat and GOAT of all time, our prototypical sporting villain and hero, our ultimate exemplars of athletic agony and ecstasy.

In the pages to follow (I have purposely, and devilishly, divided this book into 23 chapters in honor of Bobby Thomson's NY Giants jersey number), I will expose the many metaphorical dimensions of this extraordinary baseball game and its extraordinary major protagonist, Ralph Branca, one at a time, as if they were—to use two metaphors—the facets of a jewel (thus, The Game as a precious gem) or the layers of an onion being peeled back (implying the tears shed by Dodgers fans).

The title and underlying concept of this book may seem to suggest some incongruous, even nonsensical equation: Ralph Branca and the Meaning of Life indeed! Yet in fact, it does, in so many ways, make sense, because Ralph Branca and the drama that surrounded him on 10/3/51 and throughout the remainder of his life encapsulated and reflected so much of what it is like to be a human being, and to be faced with the daunting challenges life can, and does, present to all of us.

Not only do this one game and this one man possess metaphorical qualities, but so do a number of the elements—including the action on the field following the denouement, the short- and long-term consequences, even the names of the dramatis personae—surrounding it and him:

Prologue

- At the end of the game, film reveals three distinctly different (re)actions by three different players, the juxtaposition of which is powerful and revealing: Bobby's gleeful home-run trot around the bases, jumping wildly and repeatedly UP into the air; Ralph throwing his rosin bag DOWN onto the ground, just behind the bump, in anger and despair; and an always fastidious Jackie Robinson looking AHEAD just to check that Bobby touches all the bases. *Metaphors!*
- Immediately following the game, as Branca relates in his 2011 memoir, *A Moment in Time*, he is disconsolate and crushed, believing—incorrectly, of course—that he alone was solely responsible for the Dodgers' mortifying loss. As he is leaving the Polo Grounds, he meets his priest, Father Pat Rowley, with whom he discusses the "tragic" event. "But why me, Father?" Ralph asks. "I love this game so much. Why did it have to be me?" To which Father Rowley replies, "God chose you because He knew you'd be strong enough to bear this cross." *Metaphor!*
- Branca spent his entire life coming to grips, or at least attempting to do so, with his feelings about, and reactions to, "that goddamn pitch," as he so often describes it: "You know, if you kill somebody, they sentence you to life. You serve twenty years and you get paroled. I've never been paroled." So he was actually equating his tossing that fatal gopher ball with committing a murder. *Metaphor!*
- Bobby's middle name is "Brown," which is a dark color, almost black, so for Dodgers fans, he is the one wearing the figurative black hat, like the one the bad guy wore in old Western TV movies; and on the other hand, *branca* happens to be the feminine form of "white" in Portuguese (like Italian, Ralph's dad's native tongue, it is one of the five Romance languages), suggesting, for Dodgers fans, that Ralph is wearing the figurative white hat of the good guy. *Metaphors!*

In the four sections of this book, the metaphorical, emotional, and historical dimensions of The Game and the man Ralph Theodore Joseph Branca are examined: through the many past decades, the epic 10/3/51 pennant playoff game—which I watched on my 12-inch Dumont TV as a seven-year-old NY Jints fanatic—has become a metaphor for life and human experience and thus has had profound emotional effects on

Prologue

millions of rabid baseball fans (including me and Larry King) and of course on Branca himself (Part One); the phenomenon/agony of losing in sports and the role it plays and has long played in the American psyche represent the metaphorical context for some of our, and Ralph's, human flaws and limitations (Part Two); Branca's embodying of Everyman—a good man, a devout Catholic, but also a complicated person (aren't we all?) haunted his entire adult life by that one accursed fastball and the conflicts he experienced thereafter struggling with his feelings of guilt, anger, shame, and resentment—is a touching and poignant metaphor for what we all experience in our blessed but flawed lives (Part Three); and in the final chapters of the book, to put it all in perspective, I compare—and elevate, deservedly and metaphorically—Ralph (as "tragic hero," per Aristotle's definition: a good and honorable man, but a flawed one) with some of the great, conflicted protagonists of world literature: the biblical Adam and Job, Sophocles' Oedipus, Nathaniel Hawthorne's Hester Prynne, Fyodor Dostoevsky's Rodion Romanovich Raskolnikov, Franz Kafka's Josef K., and Albert Camus' Sisyphus. All metaphors for the crimes and punishments of human experience, as was, similarly in so many ways, Ralph Theodore Joseph Branca (Part Four).

Before our story (the main course) begins, I'll let you chew on, as an appetizer, a delicious baseball quote, one of my all-time favorites and, as it happens, also a delicious metaphorical malapropism. These immortal and inspiring words were uttered by Wes Westrum, former NY Giants backstop (he was behind the plate for the 10/3/51 game and also there on the cover of the 1954 inaugural edition of *Sports Illustrated*, crouching behind hitter Eddie Mathews of the Milwaukee Braves). Wes, a man not particularly renowned, shall we say, for his verbal acuity, was managing the woeful NY Mets in the mid-sixties; and in his first spring training as manager in 1966, when asked by reporters after a close game what he thought about the Mets' rare and thrilling victory, he paused for a moment, scratched his head, and replied earnestly, "It was a real cliff dweller!"

More than anything else I could possibly say, that just about sums it up.

PART ONE

Cause and Effects

First, a disclaimer: I did not know Ralph Branca personally. This book is not his biography at all, and it is not my intention to make any personal, firsthand judgments of his worth or his values as a human being.

Second, a disclaimer of the disclaimer: although I did not know Ralph Branca personally, I do know baseball, and I do know what Ralph said in his writings (especially in his memoir) and in all his interviews about the 10/3/51 game. I also know that he himself acknowledged that his life merits careful study and inspection, which is the fundamental intent of this book, even to the extent that it justifies my unabashedly ambitious title. As Branca states in the very beginning of his memoir (my italics):

Baseball is the reason I am writing this book, the reason I've led *a life worth reexamining and dissecting.*

In this opening section, I will present evidence, largely in the form of lasting memories I still retain regarding Ralph Branca and The Game and The Pitch, of the profound personal effects the classic Miracle at Coogan's Bluff game—and that one "goddamn fastball"—had on me (and, by extension, on many of us) as a baseball fanatic growing up in Brooklyn, New York; has even to this day, a full three-quarters of a century after the fact, on Giants fans like me and Dodgers fans like Larry King, who interviewed me on his TV show *Larry King Now*; and had on Branca himself, including his reaction to the subsequent cheating scandal that was revealed to the public fully a half century after the game itself transpired.

ONE

Spaldeen

Youth is wasted on the young.—George Bernard Shaw

French novelist Marcel Proust got it right: it's amazing how much we can forget during our lives and never fully recuperate through ordinary recall.

Despite the truth behind this truism, I still retain vivid memories of my childhood neighborhood, the Borough Park section of Brooklyn during the early 1950s. Then as now, Borough Park had a distinctly Hasidic flavor: her streets were punctuated by the occasional synagogue or yeshiva and chatty old men (ancient, they seemed!) attired head to foot in black and wearing long, unruly beards and *peyot*. Otherwise, it was still pretty ethnic, mostly Reform Jews and Italian Americans and the occasional Puerto Rican. The nearest Episcopalian could probably be located somewhere across the Connecticut border.

I remember the pungent smells from the peddlers' carts and the odor of sour pickles and herring in the local "appetizer" stores. And the cars parked like so many sardines on both sides of the overcrowded streets—not a sleek import in sight, but instead zaftig, red-blooded, all-American tubs whose very names have long since been banished from our collective automotive vocabulary, but that still represent for me a litany of nostalgia: DeSotos, Packards, Hudsons, Studebakers, Nashes, Kaiser-Frazers, Henry Js. I recall the stores and shops lining bustling Thirteenth Avenue: Linick's Toys (the most important one, where I purchased my beloved Spaldeens), the Schmeelk's and Hessing's luncheonettes, Ebinger's Bakery, Jaynel's Records, Moe Penn Haberdashers (men wore hats—usually fedoras—in those days), the Skilowitz and Hoffinger's delicatessens, Rothstein's Clothing, the Manny Hanny bank, The Famous vegetarian restaurant, Miller's Appetizer on the corner of Fiftieth Street (where I purchased a sour pickle straight from the barrel every day on my way home from school). Plus Al del Gaudio's Barber

Part One—Cause and Effects

Shop on Forty-ninth and G & Sons Dept. Store and the Loewe's Borough Park Theater and Monte Greenhut's Mobil Station and El-Gee Electric, all on nearby New Utrecht Avenue, nestled underneath the El tracks of the West End Line.

Ike was president, the war (the Korean one) was raging, Uncle Miltie and his Texaco Star Theater were cooking with gas on the black-and-white tube, Elvis wasn't on the scene just yet (but Eddie Fisher, Perry Como, Johnny Ray, Dean Martin, Teresa Brewer, Patti Page, and Ernie Ford were), and there were only two of everything: Fab and Tide, Colgate and Ipana, Corn Flakes and Rice Krispies, Coke and Pepsi, Crisco and Spry, Zenith and Philco. And you could buy a copy of the daily *New York Times* (or, for that matter, a pack of Topps baseball cards) for just a Buffalo nickel. Life was pretty innocent then, I suppose.

My older brother, my parents, and I lived in a tidy, two-story red brick house on Forty-ninth Street, between Twelfth and Thirteenth Avenues. Dad was a pathologist and conducted business in the front part of the house. I remember the Formica-countered laboratory with all its antediluvian paraphernalia: centrifuge machines, microscopes, slides, test tubes, pipettes, bottles, and Erlenmeyer flasks. I also recall vividly the refrigerator in the lab, in whose "Crisper" compartment he used to keep a bunch of croaking African frogs floating in water, which he used—well before the advent of test strips—for pregnancy tests.

But my most vivid childhood memories were of the games I used to play as a lunatic ballplayer. Most of my friends lived in Flatbush, so during the week, I was left to my own postschool devices. And these devices, as it turned out, were many and, at times, madly inventive. It all took place in our cement driveway. My "home court," if you will. It was, as I recall, about fifteen feet wide by about forty feet long. At one end of its length was a two-car garage with a grayish aluminum door; at the other was the street (Forty-ninth). And the two boundaries of its width were the dark-red brick side of our house and a long, dark-brown-painted wooden fence. On the other side of the fence were a junk-laden refuse area, accessible by a trap door in the fence, and a huge tar-covered rooftop surface that lay atop four or five stores on Thirteenth Avenue. That's it. No trees in the driveway, no dirt, no flora: just cement, brick, aluminum, and wood.

I spent what seemed to be many trillions of hours playing back there, between the end of school and the beginning of dinner, five days a week. And during weekends, too, when I wasn't visiting my Flatbush

ONE. *Spaldeen*

friends. And even sometimes after dinner, between dessert and pitch-blackness, when, sadly, I would have to come inside and do my homework.

It is, thus, nothing less than a miracle—based on my extensive training and dedication and experience—that I didn't eventually become a Major League Baseball Player. Of course, the subsequent intervention of my passion for tennis, the ever-increasing importance of my studies, and my diminutive stature—quick: not counting Lou Boudreau, name a great under-six-feet-tall Jewish shortstop!—all had a little something to do with the thwarting of this then-very real ambition. Plus, I was probably a lot worse than I thought I was (which was, naturally, amazing, incredible, unbelievable, perfect, the best in the entire solar system).

The tools of my trade were threefold. First, a floppy black first-sacker's mitt that came to be known as "Ollie." (Oliver J. Dragon was the mop-topped, single-toothed, long-leopard-skin-necked dragon puppet from the popular kids' TV show *Kukla, Fran, and Ollie*. He also had a floppy mouth that flapped open and shut constantly, just like my mitt.) Next, I had with me at all times my trusty Rawlings PM1 mitt, whom I called Hoover, after the vacuum-cleaner brand.

Ah, my PM1! Even today, whenever I think of it, it makes me wax poetic:

> I think it was April of '51
> that the pleading finally paid off:
> as forsythia and baseball
> begin to bloom here in Brooklyn,
> I drag my father off to Davega's
> for my very first glove.
>
> From the row of Rawlingses,
> the one on the extreme right
> beckons like a Siren.
> Succumbing, I pluck it from the company
> of its nearly identical octuplets
> as Dad plunks down a crisp Hamilton.
> (It was ten bucks, give or take,
> and worth all thousand pennies.)
>
> Like a new parent
> clinging to his precious arrival,
> I cradle mine all the way home.
> Exuding that intoxicating odor of cowhide,
> it is healthy (thank God!):

Part One—Cause and Effects

    all four fingers intact and perfectly formed,
    umbilical knot (an outie) at the base of its thumb.

    Then, the baptism.
    First, anointing it in its ritual bath,
    I perform The Soaking in Neatsfoot Oil.
    Next, the Diapering in Swaddling Twine,
    as I wrap it tightly,
    hardball tucked snugly into nascent pocket.

    With paternal pride, I watch as it grows.
    As it swallows up, with decreasing effort,
    Hardballs, softballs, tennis balls,
    Spaldeens!

    As it perfects the arts
    of shagging and snagging
    and snatching and spearing
    and scooping and smothering.
    As it darkens and softens
    and accrues character through rites of passage:
    Marks by Spikes, Soaking by Rain, Bites by Dog.

    Until, through it all, it transforms itself at last
    from glove ... into Mitt.

And, most important, my beloved Spaldeen (the Brooklynese pronunciation of the brand "Spalding"), the little pink rubber honey of a ball you could squish with your knuckles and that, when you first bought it, exuded that lovely pristine odor of "rubber powder" and fostered within you feelings of well-being and desire. More correctly, my endless succession of Spaldeens, since I was constantly losing them over the fence or on the roof.

Every cockamamy game I concocted had this in common: they were all contested between my adored New York Giants and some other NL opponent (my favorites were the Dodgers, Phillies, and Cards). They were all based on going through, to varying degrees, the batting orders of both teams in a "recreated" game (harbingers of Les Keiter). And, without exception, the Giants somehow, miraculously, always won!

First game I remember making up I called "Bottom of the Ninth." It consisted of one simple, repeated act: my throwing the Spaldeen against the garage door into an imaginary box (or, when I had chalk, I'd make four discrete dots on the imaginary corners, so my dad wouldn't discover

ONE. Spaldeen

them). That was it. After each delivery, which created a stentorian thud as rubber met aluminum, I'd convert myself into an umpire—usually Jocko Conlon or Augie Donatelli—and make a vociferous, gesticulating call. So each batter, without exception, had two options: walk or strike out. I really got into it, perfecting my crafty curve and my bullet fastball and my Hoyt Wilhelm-inspired knuckler. I would occasionally have inexplicable control problems when the Giants were up (once, I remember walking in eight runs in one inning). But when the bad guys were up, God, was I great. Virtually unhittable. And calling each pitch was great fun, too, in my squeaky, passionate adolescent ump's voice. And seeing myself mow down the heart of the order nearly every time: Furillo, Robinson, Snider, Hodges, Campanella; Ashburn, Ennis, Torgeson, Jones; Slaughter, Musial, Jablonski, Repulski—bring 'em all on, one by one. Bigger they are, harder they fall! Every game took place in the opponent's home park. Every time, of course, it came down to the bottom of the ninth. And every time—the games were typically one-run affairs—Wilhelm or Grissom would come in heroically to snuff out a last-ditch rally by The Enemy.

Then we have "Solo Stoopball," a variation of the two-man Brooklyn classic. In addition to our front stoop, we had a smallish, three-step concrete stoop leading up to the back door. This game involved pegging the Spaldeen onto the stoop, whose steps acted as batters. Throw the ball against the steps, catch it. And as usual, I'd go through both orders for nine innings, and whoever won, won (again, somehow it was always the Giants). I especially loved scooping up short hops, but my absolute favorite play was to throw the Spaldeen onto the edge of one of the steps (a "pointer"), creating a vicious, rising liner like the one Thomson hit off Branca and Pafko had to watch helplessly as it entered the left-field stands, and then make my incredible and patented "back-back-back-leap-against-the-fence-and-just-as-the-ball-is-about-to-disappear-into-the-imaginary-seats-stretch-my-pipsqueak-body-to-its-absolute-limit-and-snag-it-in-the-webbing-of-my-PM1-to-the-wild-cheering-approval-of-the-ecstatic-Giants-fans" catch.

After a spirited game of "Solo Stoopball," I'd usually go into the house for a seventh-inning-stretch snack, which consisted of either two packs of Yankee Doodles (scrumptious quasi-chocolate, creme-filled cupcakes, three to a pack) or two or three individually wrapped Devil Dogs (same deal, but hot-dog shaped), both compliments of the

Part One—Cause and Effects

immortal Drake Bakeries. And all washed down within milliseconds with a glass of all–American Borden's cow juice.

Now we come to one of my all-time favorites: "Brickball." What I remember most about this game is that I knew every nook, cranny, bump, and irregularity of the brick wall of our house against which I threw my Spaldeen in order to initiate each pitch. Ground rules: throw the ball against the wall so that it bounced back to you. You had *total* control over whether it turned out to be a grounder, squibber, bunt, short hop, liner, Texas Leaguer, popup, lazy fly, or towering drive. You just made a split decision prior to each toss, chose your Euclidean angle, and there it was. I usually made the decision based on my incredibly thorough research of each hitter, accrued through many hundreds of hours studying Bowman and Topps trading cards and box scores, as well as watching every baseball game ever televised in the history of New York. So, for instance, Ashburn would always foul off sixteen or seventeen pitches, then slap a screamer in the hole. Musial would get his token double in the gap. Ennis and Snider would blast towering drives. Against the Phils, with Ashburn leading off, I'd peg the ol' Spaldeen on an angle a few times so that it'd go foul according to my own specific, personal ground rules. Then, I'd hit a crack I knew by heart and that I knew would produce a screamer a few feet to my left and seemingly out of reach.

But no! [At this point, I put on my Ernie Harwell voice.] Here comes Hank Thompson from nowhere to snare it on the short hop ... [pause so I can short-hop it into Hoover's awaiting pocket] ... he sets ... he pegs it in the dirt ... [now I switch, in the blink of an eye, to Ollie] ... but Lockman backhands it just in time to nip the pesky lead-off hitter! ... [now I do my frenzied crowd noise] ... and the fans go *wiiiiiiiiild!*

And, as the great Linda Ellerbee would say, so it goes. Inning after inning. Grounders snared by Williams and Dark, screamers (coming at me at 196 mph from a distance of twelve feet) intercepted by Maglie and—against his will—Hamner. Short-hops gobbled up by Lockman. Grounders bobbled by Torgeson. Incredible triple plays. Drag bunts (remember them?). And, best of all, "huggers," towering flies that resulted from tossing the ball, submarine style, at a ten-degree angle off the wall, creating a tremendously high, rising arc. After perfecting this play over many thousands of hours, I was almost always able to get my Spaldeen, on its descent, to "hug" the fence just right, so that I needed to leap at the last moment to snag it (in the outer edge of the webbing, of

ONE. Spaldeen

course). I usually saved a really great one for the final out (Giants ahead by one, sacks filled with bad guys). For maximum drama, natch.

Often, in the middle of the game, I would get too bold with a "hugger," and the Spaldeen would drop tantalizingly over the fence for a round-tripper. This would happen, oh, six or seven times a game and would necessitate my climbing onto the garage roof via our backyard stone-and-red-brick barbecue, hanging onto a wobbly gutter, and hoisting myself up. Then scaling the roof, up and over to the other side, and hopping onto the roof-on-the-other-side-of-the-wooden-fence. The ball might be somewhere on that roof. Or it might have bounced to the end and down into the junk-laden refuse area. Or, worse, it might have ricocheted into a deep well (I called it "The Pit") into which I had to descend by means of a long, scary, fifteen-foot ladder—which always reminded me of the water tank where William Holden, as Sgt. Sefton, rescues a hiding-from-the-Nazis Lieutenant Dunbar (Don Taylor) in *Stalag 17*—at the bottom of which were muck and slime and a bunch of still water. In a way, I really loved these interruptive scampers because they were adventures, all part of the game, allowing me a momentary break and building up the game's suspense for when I finally wended my way back down to Earth.

And finally, there was my favorite imaginary game of all time, a special version of "Brickball" that I would play virtually every day starting on October 4, 1951, and continuing for years on end, and pretty much until I left for college in the fall of 1962. This special version I lovingly titled "Branca and Bobby." It was, of course, the precise reenactment of the "Shot Heard 'Round the World," Miracle at Coogan's Bluff game that, then and forevermore, left such an indelible mark on my psyche and in my soul.

It consisted mostly of the do-over replay of the final, glorious half-inning in all its splendor, contested with drama and gusto on the "Stoopball" stoop. I would semi-rush through the order—Alvin's bingle, Mandrake's carbon-copy bingle, Monte's popup, Whitey's double, the Mueller torn ankle, the Hartung pinch-running—to get to the crux of the matter: #23 Bobby up there twitching his bat and sweating his guts out and #13 Branca taking his windup and sweating his guts out and then the actual fateful second pitch (I chose a fastball for the opening delivery, of course, a zippy hummer right down the pipe). And each and every time, my Spaldeen, on that second fateful toss against the stoop, always exited my Branchian right hand and would always produce a

Part One—Cause and Effects

perfect "hugger" that had an odd, flat trajectory and that drove me (who had transformed myself from Branca to Pafko) back, back to The Wall, looking up forlornly, my faking mouth agape and crocodile tears forming in the corners of my eyes, as my Spaldeen flew over the fence and onto the roof and into The Pit. And then little me would pronounce, every time in the same Ernie-Harwellian voice, "It's ... *gone!*" And then Pafko, in turn, would transform himself into Bobby trotting around the imaginary bases and touching home plate amidst all his imaginary teammates: Willie, Monte, Whitey, Hank, et al. And then Bobby would transform himself into Branca, head down and throwing down the same imaginary rosin bag onto the imaginary mound and walking off the imaginary field in shame. Every day, like clockwork, "Branca and Bobby" transpired. Same drama, same schadenfreude, same joy, same result.

All these feverish Spaldeen games would last for hours, especially with Ashburn fouling off all those pitches and the painfully, joyously detailed reenactment of the 10/3/51 contest. And they'd have lasted well into the night were it not for either of two interruptive phenomena: Game Called Due to Parking (my dad would drive his two-toned-green Chrysler smack into the middle of the field: imagine!) or else Game Postponed Due to Mom Announcing Dinner.

When I finally came in, unwillingly and with great remorse, I remember always having to employ a bar of gritty Lava soap to eradicate my equally gritty "badges of honor": sweat from playing, grime from climbing, grit from "The Pit," and dirt from the appetizer backyard.

After I washed up, and as I sat down for a delightful meal of salmon croquettes and succotash or some other indigestible gourmet offering (of course, the Yankee Doodles or Devil Dogs had left

The beloved "Spaldeen."

16

ONE. *Spaldeen*

little room in my tummy for any kind of further gastric consumption), and all through dinner, and all through homework, and up until the time—between the dental application of brusha-brusha-brusha Ipana and Mr. Sandman—when I finally fell asleep, all I could think of, all I could fill my little idiot's brain with, in those wondrous, halcyon, solipsistic days of my youth, was how, with the help of my beloved Spaldeen, the amazing Jints were gonna eke out yet another series of glorious victories in the driveway, especially at the culmination of "Branca and Bobby," tomorrow afternoon, starting at three o'clock sharp.

TWO

Bedroom

It's ... gone!—Ernie Harwell

On this overcast Wednesday afternoon of October 3, 1951, my little bedroom in my family's modest two-story house in Brooklyn, New York, resembles a crowded wing in Cooperstown. Carpet and walls are barely visible, nearly every available inch of every surface hidden by a vast and colorful collage of team pennants and programs, scorecards, yearbooks, autographs, photographs, buttons, caps, baseballs, carefully cut-out *New York Times* box scores, and of course my trusty Rawlings PM1 baseball mitt and his loyal mittmate Ollie.

The centerpiece of the LBMBM (Little Bobby Mitchell Baseball Museum) occupies its usual position in the middle of the carpet, namely, a "Log Book" with a black-and-white-flecked cover bursting at the seams from its overstuffed contents, ninety-six pages of baseball cards (Topps and Bowman), painstakingly collected, each card attached lovingly by seven-year-old me with LePage's Gripspreader Mucilage Glue and arranged with excruciating exactitude, team (NL first) after team (then AL) and in descending order (by batting averages and ERAs), all these little 3½" × 2½" rectangles of cardboard depicting ballplayers frozen in stupefyingly fake poses, some making imaginary catches, some pitching imaginary balls, still others staring catatonically into space with bats posed gently against shoulders, futilely awaiting a fastball or an Uncle Charlie that they know will never arrive. My favorites are the fake poses of all my beloved NY Jints, which I have segregated and presented at the beginning of the book and—different from the other fifteen MLB teams—alphabetized painstakingly, from Bamberger (George) to Yvars (Sal).

In the spirit of baseball-card sentimentality, I feel the need to pause briefly here, to fast-forward eleven years later, and to recount—with no small degree of melancholy—the tragic fate of my beloved collection....

TWO. Bedroom

YOU DID ... WHAT?!!!!!?
The fateful year was 1962. Wednesday, October 3, to be exact. Eleven years to the day—if you can believe it!—of the Bobby Thomson– Ralph Branca Miracle Game. And (give or take an exclamation point) this was my precise reaction when I learned of the Dastardly Deed from my mother's own lips. Of the devastating news that she had disposed of my entire baseball-card collection, somehow blithely tossing it right into the garbage can. Lock, stock, and proverbial barrel. A cold, cruel premeditated act of extermination, complete with malice aforethought.
My own mother!
Which begs the deeply disturbing metaphysical question: how could the very same person who went through the pain and torment of nine months of gestation plus the actual delivery of a human being, as well as the formative nurturing of this same human, commit such an egregious felony against that offspring, a crime of such towering magnitude and heinousness as to affect his entire life and deprive him of riches (emotional and fiduciary) beyond measure?

Just as I suspected. You *have* no answer. How could you? The question is transparently rhetorical and thus defies a reasonable response. It's just like asking, "How could Medea have slain her own flesh and blood?" or "How could Ralph have stuck with the fastball on his second pitch to Bobby?"

Through time (it has been over six decades since The Deed was committed), I have replayed what I assume and imagine to have been The Actual Act over and over and over in my mind, in a vain attempt to make some sense of it; but all my efforts have proven—alas—to be to no avail. Fruitless. Futile. Abortive.

Here's how my reenactment of The Crime goes. I'm away at college, freshman year. And there's my mother at home, doing her usual twice-a-day cleanup of my (old but newly abandoned) room. Dusting. Sweeping. And, naturally, rearranging. And generally making the room look presentable (in case, of course, the president of the United States or Queen Elizabeth should just happen to be strolling through the Hasidic Borough Park section of Brooklyn, of a Thursday afternoon, and had the urge to pop in). I'd left a number of personal possessions at home, which I assumed were—legally and otherwise—still my personal possessions and would remain untouched until I myself might decide to jettison them. Or not.

Anyway, there's Mom rearranging, and she suddenly spies, on a

Part One—Cause and Effects

shelf in my bookcase, three or four overstuffed and impressive-looking Composition Books. You know the kind: those "logbooks" with the funny black-and-white-speckled covers that we used for penmanship in grade school in days of yore. The kind people used for important stuff, official stuff, private stuff. *Overstuffed with what?*, you might ask. Why, with an exceedingly large amount of baseball cards. Cards I'd been collecting painstakingly for, oh, maybe a dozen years. Cards arranged in excruciating order, alphabetically and according to teams and batting averages and ERAs. And what else is lying there on the shelf just minding its own business? Nothing less than five or six shoeboxes, brimming to the top, about to explode from their own plenitude. And sticking out of which are baseball cards that just can't be held in check. Wildly, energetically thrusting themselves outward, as if crying to be deposited in ... yet another shoebox! Well, these invaluable and important-looking artifacts sure look exactly like—for all the world and to the naked, untrained eye—*things you'd never in your wildest dreams imagine someone could, knowingly or unknowingly, dispose of, toss out, or otherwise contemplate trashing.*

So there's Mom innocently dusting and rearranging one Wednesday afternoon. When, suddenly, spying all these important-looking artifacts and inspecting them for a fleeting second, she presumably whispers to herself, "Hmmm, these could be important artifacts and maybe they mean something to my dear, wonderful, now-departed son. And after all, they *are* in his room and they *are* still his very own private possessions, even though he's flown from the nest. And boy, it sure looks like he's invested a whole lot of time lovingly arranging, collecting, and hoarding them. And he *is* a baseball nut, so they're probably still very dear to his heart. And, you know, it would probably be inappropriate to throw them all out without at least consulting him, without having the human decency and the courtesy to ask him personally whether he'd like to keep them or to have me throw them in the garbage. And I happen to know he spent hours and hours with them, starting when he was a little kid, so I'm guessing they probably still mean a great deal to him, physically, emotionally, and spiritually. And look! Look at all these cute little 3½" × 2½" cardboard cards that used to give him so much pleasure! Cards that he spent many of the joyful hours of his youth arranging in these logbooks and keeping in these shoeboxes! Cards that he used to take out on special occasions (like when the sun came up in the morning) to flip endlessly on the carpeted floor of his bedroom (heads or tails) or against his bedroom wall (leaners)!

TWO. Bedroom

And look! [She flips through the cards in one of the shoeboxes.] Look at all his favorite cards and players! Why, there's Coot Veal and Cot Deal and Turk Lown and old, wizened Alpha Brazle and Sibby Sisti and Sam Jethroe and Herm Wehmeier and Bud Podbielan and Don Mossi and Roy Smalley and Johnny Klippstein and Billy Loes and Duane Pillette and Luke Easter and Roy Sievers and Matt Batts and Phil Cavarretta and Chris Van Cuyk and Johnny Wyrostek and Dave Jolly and Virgil Jester (I know he got a kick out of the fact that these two funnymen were on the same team) and Stan Palys and Peanuts Lowrey and Solly Hemus and all his beloved Giants (even Tookie Gilbert and Sal Yvars and Max Lanier and Alex Konikowski) and Wayne Terwilliger and Eddie Yost the Walking Man and ageless Minnie Miñoso and Ned Garver and Erv Palica and Sid Hudson and Ike Delock and Ferris Fain and Gus Zernial and Al Zarilla and Granny Hamner and bespectacled Earl Torgeson and Carlos Paula and Reno Bertoia and Saul Rogovin and Dee Fondy and Clint Courtney and Vinegar Bend Mizell! [Now she puts her right index finger, ever-so-thoughtfully, against her pursed lips.] And ... naaaaaaaah, he probably doesn't want them anymore, and besides, they look like junk!" And so, without a second's thought, without a glimmer of hesitation or even guilt, she gathers them all up in her arms, all three or four overstuffed Composition Books and all five or six impressive-looking shoeboxes, and lugs them to the garbage can outside in the alley. And there, with no earthly witnesses to gaze upon this Unspeakable Act of Mass Destruction, she tosses them guiltlessly and remorselessly into the can and, with that innocent, sweet smile of hers, returns to complete her various Duties of Cleanliness and Godliness.

Well, there it is. Every time I replay The Awful Act in my mind, the exact chronology, specific description, and precise movements are always the same, never changing a whit, just as I have just painfully described them. And for many years (when I was younger and more cynical), I would hold The Deed against my mother (can you imagine?) and bring it up occasionally (how insensitive!) and make her feel guilty (a pox on me!). Yep, in my more immature days, I was under the impression that, were I still in possession of my entire baseball-card collection, I could get a bundle for it if I put it up for sale. And maybe I could retire early and buy my own remote Mediterranean island and spend the rest of my days leisurely reading Proust and painting majestic landscapes and playing the ocarina and swinging on my hammock while being fed grapes by my large, attentive staff....

Part One—Cause and Effects

But those days are long gone, and I am over my anger and grief at the loss of my priceless cardboard buddies. All that's left is the haunting, repeated imaginary reconstruction of how my mother could ever have committed The Senseless, Murderous Deed.

In my deepest moments of self-examination, I occasionally muse about one other thing. Over the past six decades, I've met a very great number of men of my generation who, like me, happen to be lifelong baseball fanatics. And who, like me, happen to have had (for their own private pleasure, and eons before fantasy baseball was ever conceived) immense, invaluable baseball-card collections kept in logbooks and shoeboxes and arranged in excruciating order, alphabetically and according to teams and batting averages and ERAs. And who, like me, had maternal relatives who, without a trace of guilt or remorse, violently exterminated their entire card collections, tossing them into the garbage can in the alley. And I wonder to myself whether all these Terrible Deeds were in fact just coincidental: isolated acts that just happened to occur all the time, decade after decade. Or maybe, just maybe, they occurred far too frequently and in too many geographic and demographic areas and over too long a time and to too many unsuspecting young men just going off to college to be unrelated.

And the more I wonder, the more convinced I am that there are actually three phenomena that you can absolutely count on in life: death, taxes, and your mother accidentally tossing out your entire baseball-card collection. Lock, stock, and proverbial barrel.

Now back to October 3, 1951. On this particular and extraordinary Wednesday afternoon three-quarters of a century ago, surrounded in my bedroom by all my baseball memorabilia and paraphernalia, my seven-year-old eyes are glued to the Lilliputian screen of my black-and-white Dumont TV, its twelve-inch surface dwarfed by a hunk of a hexagonal mahogany frame and flanked on its right by a weird-looking circular knob that you turned around and around until it settled on any one of seven—*seven!*—channels: 2, 4, 5, 7, 9, 11, 13. All bathed, funny enough, in a brightly lit background of orange and black, the very colors of my own NY Jints.

As the merits of Chesterfield cigarettes are being trumpeted on the TV ("Smells milder, tastes milder, plus no unpleasant aftertaste"), young me is attempting to get his wits together and his spirits up, with my Giants hopelessly trailing the Detested Bums, 4–1, at the Polo Grounds in the last-licks bottom of the ninth in the third and deciding game of the NL pennant playoff series.

TWO. Bedroom

On channel 11, WPIX, the most important contest in the long and glorious history of America's national pastime and also of my incipient existence is wrapping up. Being only seven, I don't yet appreciate this historically, but I for sure sense it emotionally, right in the core of my preadolescent NY Giants fan's heart.

For the past six months, I have been living through a historic baseball season, the whole drama of a pennant race between the two New York City National League archrival clubs, my beloved New York Giants and the despicable Brooklyn Dodgers. Behind by thirteen-and-a-half games on August 11, my Jints improbably stormed back by winning thirty-seven of their final forty-four games and to my total delight caught the odious Bums on the last day, the Dodgers only surviving and earning a playoff date against their Hated Enemy thanks to the final-game heroics of who else but Jack Roosevelt Robinson, who almost single-handedly beat the Phillies by stabbing a low liner off the bat of Eddie Waitkus (he of the rifle-shot-to-the-chest incident) in the bottom of the twelfth inning with the bases jammed, then hitting a solo homer in the top of the fourteenth against future Hall of Famer Robin Roberts to win it, 9–8.

And so, after the Giants beat the Dodgers in the opener of the best-of-three National League pennant playoff, 3–1, and the Dodgers stormed back to win the second, 10–0, here I sit in front of my twelve-inch Dumont watching my beloved Giants in the deciding game, trailing by 4–1 in the bottom of the ninth, with the Giants down to their final three, puny outs.

Up to the plate strides Alvin Dark, number nineteen with his trademark black bat, who in his past was a pretty-boy quarterback at LSU and in his future will be accused of being a racist.

"C'mon, Newk, *toss him a fat one!*" I scream to Don Newcombe, the brawny Brooklyn hurler inside the TV screen, my voice now hoarse from preadolescent passion.

Innocence is bliss, and life for me seems so simple now, so Manichaean: just like in the TV Westerns, you got your good guys and you got your bad guys, the guys in the white hats and the guys in the black hats.

And if you have faith, you will end up happily ever after.

And if you wish hard enough for the good guys to win, they do!

Which is precisely why I have not given up, I will never give up, and anything can happen, even miracles, right?

And then.

Part One—Cause and Effects

Dark bleeds a single off the glove of 1B Gil Hodges, and Don Mueller follows suit with another bleeder to nearly the identical spot.

"How come you were guarding the line and keeping Alvin close to the bag instead of positioning yourself for the double play?" I ask Gil rhetorically and sardonically through the TV screen. "That would've been a DP, and there would've been two outs. But thanks, dear Gil!"

Giants on first and third now, and we're still down by three but still three outs to go, and hey, ya never know, I am thinking.

The always dependable Monte Irvin steps up to the plate now, to continue the last-ditch rally. My Giants' candle is still flickering, but barely.

"C'mon, Monte, maybe walk to fill the sacks or sock a homer to tie the game," I plead to the future Hall of Famer.

To my horror, the overanxious Irvin fouls out meekly to Hodges, and sadly, the Giants are now down to their final two measly outs and it's almost curtains for the good guys and now it's all up to Whitey Lockman and then Bobby Thomson on deck.

And Whitey flails at a high, outside pitch and somehow strokes a scorcher over third past Billy Cox and just inside the foul line and into the corner and left fielder Andy Pafko chases it down and Dark scores and Lockman breezes into second and Mueller tears his ankle to shreds barreling, slideless, into third and Clint Hartung runs for him and Dodgers pitcher Big Don Newcombe, virtually unhittable until this point, appears to be toast.

And now it's 4–2 Dodgers with Giants on second and third and Bobby Thomson coming up and for the first time all game a bright and totally true ray of hope illuminates my Manichaean concept of Life as a TV Western. Good guys with the white hats win, bad guys with the black hats lose. I croak—remotely—to opposing manager Charlie Dressen: "Bring Branca in! Bring 'im *in*," my incipient encyclopedic baseball memory recalling that the next batter, Bobby Thomson, had already hit a two-run shot off the Dodger fireballer in the opening playoff game.

As luck would have it, Dressen somehow heeds my plea and brings in number 13, big Ralph Branca. And here comes the Flying Scot, Robert Brown Thomson, to the plate with the score 4–2 and I slouch farther down in my little brown wooden chair in front of my twelve-inch Dumont and bite my lower lip, in incandescent hope, until it bleeds.

"C'mon, Ralphie boy," I whisper, "give 'im a big fat one." *Bran-ca* ...

TWO. Bedroom

Bran-ca ... Bran-ca, I scream inside my head, as if my very life depended on the brawny reliever's messing up.

And Bobby takes a strike right down the pike and all seven-year-old me is praying for is another heater down Main Street....

And now Branca winds up and delivers and, as luck would have it, he somehow heeds my plea and darned if it's not another fastball and it's up and in and out of the strike zone but wait, Bobby catches it just right and—

Crack!

Bobby tomahawks it good and instinctively I *know* and the Spalding cowhide orb is bludgeoned by the Adirondack ash bat and the ball takes off on a vicious low trajectory and I watch hopefully while Dodgers left fielder Andy Pafko watches helplessly as the topspin from Bobby's mighty uppercut swing transports the ball over Andy's head and buries it in section 35 of the lower left-field stands.

Amid the chaos of the crowd emanating from my Dumont twelve-inch screen and the shock and awe and disbelief of innocent bystander seven-year-old me: an exclamation point proffered by Giants TV announcer, the future Hall of Famer Ernie Harwell, a ruthlessly pithy, bisyllabic call that is uplifting in its utter simplicity and stark revelation of reality.

"It's ... *gone!*"

Two little words, two tiny syllables. To die-hard Giants fans like me, though, they might as well have sprouted an extra syllable and morphed magically into "Hope prevails!" or "Life is good!" or ... "Miracle!"

"It's ... *gone!*"

Gone are the Detestable Dodgers' chances of going to the Series.

Gone are my doubts concerning self-belief and my fears of impending doom.

Gone is my lack of total faith in unlikely, unforeseen miracles.

All the faith I had placed in these grown-up idols and heroes and role models has been somehow improbably confirmed by the nexus of the strong but fallible right arm of instant goat Ralph Branca and the potent ash weapon of instant GOAT Bobby Thomson.

These gods in flannel, my own divine New York Giants, have just come through and allowed me to believe, for the very first time, in All Things Wonderful and Possible.

And for the very first time in my pristine life, Victory is suddenly, gorgeously snatched from the jaws of Defeat.

Part One—Cause and Effects

It is, in fact, my first exposure to all those Future Expressions of Hey-Ya-Never-Know and Possibility and Hope: "Que sera, sera" (predating Doris Day) and "It ain't over till it's over" (predating Yogi) and "Don't give up ... don't ever give up" (predating Jimmy Valvano).

As I watch the euphoric ending of this iconic battle on my 12-inch Dumont—on October 3, 1951, at precisely 3:58 p.m. Eastern time—I only have eyes for one solitary figure: Bobby Thomson, number 23, the Flying Scot, (aptly) flying around the bases, as vertical through leaps of joy as he is horizontal in his magical journey touching all the bases.

There he is, Superhero Bobby Thomson, from Staten Island via Scotland, romping around the bases, his body bounding forward and bouncing ferociously up and down, up and down, now rounding third, passing manager Leo Durocher who's going bananas and berserk, then gleefully gliding home, mobbed at the dish by his jubilant teammates: there's Whitey and Willie and Monte and Alvin....

On the other hand, preadolescent, rabid Jints fan me has no awareness whatsoever of the flip side of the proverbial coin, of the losing, deflated Dodgers players on the field, of the desolate and lonely Andy Pafko ("Pafko at the Wall," as Don DeLillo so aptly put it), of the vigilant and hypercompetitive Jackie Robinson making damn sure Bobby touches every single frigging base, and most of all of, most of all, the lone figure of Ralph Theodore Joseph Branca: spirits and hopes and dreams dashed by his tragic gaffe, his woefully misguided fastball, head down in despair and dejection, slamming the rosin bag down onto the ground beyond the mound in disgust and anger and angst. It will only be many decades later, when I study the postdinger video closely and the still shots of the infield, that I show any shred of empathy and realize what Dodgers fans must have been feeling, and the tragic side of what for me, as a Giants fanatic, was, on that overcast early October afternoon in 1951, pure comic relief. And what this moment must have felt like for Ralph Branca, for whom I never felt a drop of pity or even compassion or empathy on 10/3/51 but have since developed said feelings lo these many decades later.

It is this figure—Ralph Branca, one of the two major protagonists of that iconic game and the person whose life was most profoundly affected by it—of whom seven-year-old me was then totally and blissfully unaware (blinded as I was by the rabidity of my rooting for my NY Giants) and who, ironically, has dominated my thoughts about this formative sporting event ever since I became of age: it is this figure who

TWO. Bedroom

Black-and-white Dumont television (1951).

is now the crux and central protagonist of, and the axis upon which rotates, the book you are now holding in your hands.

After all that joyous dust settles, I turn off my Dumont, and a silence fills my little room, a deafening and unfamiliar quietude of a species I have never before experienced. I am agog, bewildered, dumbstruck, speechless. And I suddenly realize my own human, hopeful, smiling potential at this ridiculously tender age. Because literally, in nickname, and, now, figuratively....

I *am* Bobby!

But my joy and optimism and positive view of life and of all its possibilities, feelings that will remain with me for the rest of my born days, are only half of this grand metaphorical baseball and life story. And I would not, and certainly not truly, discover the other half of that emotional spectrum—from the opposite, soured, negative, pessimistic, even cynical perspective of the millions of rabid Brooklyn Dodgers fans who were so deeply affected by that one "goddamn pitch" tossed by Ralph Branca—until a full sixty-seven years later, when this story, this journey, transported me in the very strangest of ways from Bedroom to Green Room.

THREE

Green Room

Damn near killed me, that Branca fastball!—Larry King

According to Yiddish guru Leo Rosten, a *mentsh* (yes, that is the preferred spelling) is described as an upright, honorable, and decent person. This is also a fitting description, as far as I could tell, of the late Larry King.

I say this based on personal experience. My contact with Larry began in 2007, when I called his manager cold and out of the blue, explaining to her what Larry and I had in common (both were born in Brooklyn, both have had a lifelong passion for baseball, both have had coronary bypass surgery) and asking her to please ask him if he would be so kind as to write a blurb for my recently completed baseball novel, *Once Upon a Fastball*. When I hung up the phone, I was pretty certain that this was a really long shot, and that even though I had at that point published eight books and had established a decent publishing track record, I was by no means a "household name" and who was I, a relative unknown, to ask the iconic Larry King to say something nice about my novel but then again hey ya never know (a lesson first learned on 10/3/51, of course)? To my surprise and shock, a few weeks later, I received a call from his manager informing me that certainly Larry would be more than happy to write a blurb for the baseball novel, which he did.

A *mentsh* is an upright, honorable, and decent person.

Larry did write something (very) nice about my novel, and the blurb actually appeared on the front of the book jacket, and that was that, until ten years later, in the spring of 2017. It was then that I was finishing work on a memoir (*Time for a Heart-to-Heart: Reflections on Life in the Face of Death*) based on my 2015 heart transplant and I decided, what the heck, to ask Larry to write not just a blurb, but the foreword for the book, not knowing if he would remember me and our coronary/

THREE. Green Room

Brooklyn/baseball commonalities from a decade ago. Sure enough, he remembered me and graciously agreed to write it, which he did.

A *mentsh* is an upright, honorable, and decent person.

After the memoir was published the September of 2017, I had the utter gall and audacity to contact the producer of Larry's TV interview show, *Larry King Now*, asking her if he would be so kind as to interview me (*me!*) on his show, thinking who was I, a relative unknown, asking the iconic Larry King to interview me, but then again hey ya never know? Sure enough, he remembered me and graciously agreed to interview me, which he did about six months later.

A *mentsh* is an upright, honorable, and decent person.

And so, it was not until 67 years—between 1951 and 2018—after I watched the iconic Giants/Dodgers, Thomson/Branca, Miracle at Coogan's Bluff game on my Dumont black-and-white 12-inch TV that, at least for twenty intensely revealing minutes, I get a real glimpse into what the opposite side, the true-blue (literally and figuratively) Dodgers fan was suffering at that very time while I was joyfully embracing the entire intoxicating experience. And what he thought of the source of so much angst and disappointment for him and all those millions of other Dodgers fans, namely, the author of that "goddam fastball," Ralph Branca.

Jints and Bums. The Ecstasy and the Agony. Bobby and Ralph. Me and Larry. My bedroom to his green room. Awesome.

After I arrive at Larry's TV recording studio in LA, his producer welcomes me and my wife, Susan Love, and leads us into the green room, where, I assume, the two of us would wait until it was time to get made up and miked up before the interview in the main area of the studio.

Never assume anything.

Barely had Susan and I sat down and caught our breaths, when in strolls Larry the *mentsh*, nattily clad in his iconic suspenders (navy blue in this case), dark trousers, dark sneakers, a pink dress shirt, and a warm orange-and-blue paisley necktie. He is also sporting a warm smile.

"So, Bob, how's the ticker doin'?"

"Pretty good, Larry, can't complain," I reply. "Yours?"

"No complaints. So, Susan, how ya doin'? Hope you don't mind, but Bob and I need to talk a little baseball before the interview...."

And for the next twenty minutes, indeed we do. And quality baseball shmooz (yes, that is the preferred spelling, per Leo Rosten) it is.

Part One—Cause and Effects

Our short time together in the green room is quite amazing and stimulating and passionate, especially chatting so intensely with Larry before the interview and defusing whatever nervousness I am feeling. In fact, we basically stuff about 150 years of our collective baseball knowledge and fanaticism into those 1,200-or-so precious seconds.

At first, it is all about baseball trivia. As leadoff hitter and due to Larry's profound baseball knowledge, I know I need to ask him something esoteric and oddball to start things rolling, so I choose one of my favorites: "Which pitcher had the best W–L percentage in his first full three years in the majors, beating second-place Cy Young by nearly 100 percentage points?" I query.

"Dunno, who?"

"Salvatore Anthony Maglie," I tell him. "The pride of Niagara Falls. My fave player, aside from Willie. Years ago, I even named my Rhodesian Ridgeback Maglie!"

"Yeah, Sal Maglie. The Barber. Last of fourteen players to play for NY Giants, NY Yankees, and Brooklyn Dodgers," Larry adds, correctly of course, then asking (it's his turn), "Who was the only athlete to hit a homer off Sandy Koufax and catch a TD pass from Y.A. Tittle?"

Right off the bat (sorry), I know I have to make a tough decision: show diplomacy and deference or demonstrate my supreme knowledge? I had encountered this factoid somewhere in the distant past and actually knew that it was incorrect: the presumed answer, Alvin Dark, did indeed hit a homer off Sandy but couldn't have caught a TD pass from Tittle, who had attended LSU as a quarterback after Dark had left that fine institute of learning. Not wishing to correct him, and not having the inclination to contradict or ruffle feathers or to appear to be undiplomatic or disrespectful, I take the high road, in deference to Larry's professional stature and our incipient camaraderie, and reply, "I dunno, who?"

"Alvin ... *Dark*," Larry says with a satisfied smile and carefully pausing before, and then enunciating, the third and final syllable.

After several more minutes of spirited and competitive trivia, and after we discover we are both Scorpios, we alternate sharing old baseball memories: my dad catching a foul ball off the bat of Giants second baseman Davey Williams in a 1954 Giants-Bosox exhibition game at the Polo Grounds he took me to on 6/28/54; Larry's encounter, as a junior journalist in the late 1940s, with foul-mouthed sonuvabitch manager Leo Durocher.... And then a few minutes more about the cowboy-movie

THREE. Green Room

mentality of the '40s and '50s, the Good Guys in the white hats (especially Tex Ritter) and the Bad Guys (the "outlaws") in the black ones. And his—still, at 16—watching Happy Felton's Knot Hole Gang on Channel 9 and his beloved Bums (even down to George "Shotgun" Shuba; the Jewish Cal Abrams; the pitcher with the anti–Semitic-sounding name Chris Van Cuyk; and second-stringer Rube Walker, who actually was the starting catcher in the 10/3/51 game because Campy was injured) and my beloved Jints (even down to my three "K guys": starting pitcher Dave Koslo, after whom I named my yellow Lab; relief pitcher Jack Kramer—no, not the tennis guy; and reliever Alex Konikowski, who had maybe the widest batting stance in the history of the game).

All this leads up to—out of the blue, but not really—a spirited discussion of the single event in baseball history that seemed to shape our respective formative years, in quite different but unsurprisingly identical ways: that one goddam fastball Branca threw to Thomson on 10/3/51 at precisely 3:58 p.m. Eastern time. A life-changing event of such behemoth proportions, it turns out, that we are still now thinking about it, discussing it, comparing mental notes on it, sixty-seven years after the fact. One single baseball game. *One single goddam pitch.*

There were so many seemingly existential and unanswered questions, illogical actions, and unpredictable results for me and Larry to sort through during these few intense moments together. So many enigmas! *Why? Why? Why?* Why'd Sukeforth tell Dressen to send in Branca in relief of Newk? (One curve in the dirt?) Why didn't Branca walk Thomson intentionally? (Bobby's homer off him in Game 1 of series, right?) And get to scared rookie Willie Mays in the on-deck circle? (Willie, who was much less an RBI threat against Ralph than Bobby?) Why'd Branca throw Bobby a fastball on that second pitch? (Wasn't Bobby, in Ralph's mind, naturally waiting for the curve after the hummer on pitch #1?)

Unbeknownst to me, these were the subliminal literary and motivational seeds—sown into my green-room, highly stimulated brain—of the book you are now reading.

The effects these issues had on our young (in 1951) psyches, however, was the topic Larry and I end up discussing the most intensely: how much The Game and The Pitch changed my life as a Giants fan and my perspective as a human being in my formative years and how much The Game and The Pitch nearly ruined Larry's, as a seventeen-year-old person and as a die-hard Dodgers fan. And the expression *changed our*

Part One—Cause and Effects

lives is not hyperbole, but rather, it actually and graphically describes how this game affected the trajectory of our young existences, and in the same way those of millions of baseball fans, Giants and Dodgers alike. It formed our two different ways of looking at the world and thinking about the world—then and for years to come: Hope vs. Cynicism, Certitude vs. Doubt, Ecstasy vs. Agony, Gratitude vs. Anger, Contentment vs. Envy—all evinced, simultaneously, by the very same spectacle, the very same single pitch. They are two sides of the same coin, we agree, the yinyang, two pieces of evidence that sometimes life can be a zero-sum game, with winners and losers canceling each other out and leaving nothing at all in between.

At one (charmingly vulnerable) point, Larry confesses to me that at the age of 17, he was listening to Red Barber's radio broadcast on WMGM-AM, just as I was watching Ernie Harwell's TV broadcast on WPIX. He tells me that at the moment Bobby's homer disappeared into the left-field stands, "I felt as if I had just *died*" and then, "Damn near killed me, that Branca fastball!" To which I respond, "Funny, because it was the first time I felt, deep inside, that I was really *alive*." We also discuss a similar reaction to Larry's felt by a common friend, the late Dick Schaap, the pioneering sportswriter who was Larry's contemporary and my occasional tennis doubles partner: "When Bobby Thomson hit the home run, my childhood ended."

The actual interview about my heart-transplant memoir goes predictably smoothly (just as our green-room chat had: Larry was a great listener, he asked the right questions, and we enjoyed each other's company) and is actually both fun and cathartic. But I could never get out of my mind, during the interview and ever since, the intensity and even the intimacy of my *pre-interview* chat with Larry, our chat largely about him and me and Ralph.

As Susan and I drive back southward from Larry's LA studio to our home in Carlsbad (a drive of about an hour and a half), my mind is in a frenzy, reviewing, musing about, and ruminating on the multifarious topics Larry and I had discussed in the green room just an hour or two before.

I realize how fortuitous this pre-interview time spent with Larry was: how Ralph Branca had posthumously (he had passed a year or so before the interview) been the glue of an unexpected bond between Larry and me, two total strangers originally brought together, funny enough, by my dying, then refurbished and transplanted heart. Funny

THREE. Green Room

Larry King and Bob Mitchell in LA TV studio, 2018 (photograph by Susan Ellen Love).

enough, because my heart was similarly, but figuratively, moribund but then refurbished following the Branca "goddam pitch," while at the same time Larry's was, figuratively, buoyant but then moribund as a result of that very same fastball.

And then, immediately following this rumination, as creative

Part One—Cause and Effects

thoughts often do, a sudden epiphany barges into my brain, about the pre-interview and where it took place, which I jot down feverishly in my writing journal the instant I cross the threshold of our house upon our return from LA....

The *Green* Room!

I am now having an odd thought, maybe even a silly one. Or maybe, on second thought, not so silly? It has to do with the room Larry and I and Susan were in when we first met just a few hours ago. The *green room. Green!* And it suddenly occurs to me that the two extremes of sentient feeling Larry and I discussed regarding The Game and The Pitch are perfectly and simultaneously suited to this very same color, and its traditional symbolism, which includes both ends of the "feeling" spectrum: on the one hand, green can symbolize *jealousy* (in Shakespeare's *The Merchant of Venice*, Portia refers to "green-eyed jealousy"; in *Othello*, Iago refers to jealousy as a "green-eyed monster"; and then there's the expression "to be green with envy") and also another negative feeling, *shame*. And on the other, it can symbolize *hope* and other positive feelings: growth, rebirth, healing, and renewal.

Hope, growth, rebirth, healing, and renewal were feelings awakened on 10/3/51, at the crack of Bobby's bat, for me, for millions of Giants fans, and of course for GOAT Bobby Thomson. And, at the same time, jealousy (wishing that the Dodgers and not the Giants had won that crucial and deciding pennant game) and shame were feelings suffered by Larry, by millions of Bums fans, and of course by goat Ralph Branca.

FOUR

Echoing Green

We wuz robbed!—Max Schmeling's fight manager Joe Jacobs

Speaking of Giant things, it's now time—sooner than later—to discuss the Elephant in the Room, namely, the cheating scandal surrounding The Game and The Pitch that for the past quarter century has sullied, and hung as a specter over, the Giants' epic victory and supplied Ralph Branca with an excuse and a scapegoat and had a pachydermatous effect on the psyches and the legacies of both Bobby and Ralph.

This is complicated. But then again, so is life.

The Giants scandal, and how it affected Ralph Branca's life in particular, is a debate that contains within it two contrapuntal arguments worthy of contemplation and discussion. It is a debate the conclusions to which are, frustratingly, nearly impossible to resolve and quite possibly moot. It is a debate about which, for the past quarter century, writers have spilled, as they say, much ink.

It all began to be unraveled fully (although prior to this there were certainly suspicions of malfeasance) in 2001 as the brainchild of journalist Joshua Prager in the form of a *Wall Street Journal* piece he wrote, fifty years after the game. Five years later, Prager followed up the piece with a meticulously researched and brilliantly presented tome titled *The Echoing Green*, in which he revealed in all its (in)glory and in painstaking detail the machinations behind the scandal.

Although the details have been rehashed over the past twenty-five years, I will re-rehash them briefly at the outset, for clarity's sake.

The following is my attempt to reconsider the facts of the scandal revealed through Prager's indefatigable sleuthing in the context of this section of the book upon which you are now embarking, which considers how this "cause" affected Ralph Branca and his psyche, and how he reacted to it.

To begin with, here is the presentation of the cause, that is, the

Part One—Cause and Effects

specific details of the side of the debate that justifies Branca's argument based on what is indisputable and undebatable:

- The Giants used a complex network of spies and a telescope to steal the Dodgers' signs and allow the Giants not only to come roaring back after being behind the Dodgers by thirteen-and-a-half games in August, but also to steal the pennant by telling Bobby Thomson which pitch was coming after that first called-strike fastball;
- Leo Durocher, the admittedly fiery and win-at-all-costs Giants manager, hatched the concept of the entire sign-stealing scheme;
- To steal the signals from opposing catchers, the Giants used a 35mm Wollensak telescope in the clubhouse behind center field, used by infielder Hank Schenz, then third-base coach Herman Franks;
- The Giants used a wire (laid by Abraham Chadwick, ironically a die-hard Dodgers fan!) to relay the signal from the clubhouse to the bullpen, the only one in the majors in fair territory;
- The wire led to a buzzer that buzzed in the bullpen: 1 buzz for a fastball, 2 for a curve;
- In the Giants' bullpen, backup catcher Sal Yvars listened to the buzzer and then would hold up a baseball to indicate to the batter that a fastball was coming, or toss it in the air for a breaking ball; and
- The Giants had this primitive yet elaborate Rube-Goldberg sign-stealing system in place starting on July 20, 1951, as confessed by Franks and Yvars to Prager while he was researching his book.

The counterpoint to this is the side of the debate that represents Ralph Branca's very human reaction to the scandal, his feeling of relief and then his use of it as a scapegoat, a welcome excuse for blame and for avoidance of taking full responsibility for his action (despite numerous honest attempts to do so through patience and temperance).

I should add that although I'm not sure that the proverbial pen is mightier than the proverbial sword, the power of the pen is indeed awesome, so consequently I have avoided any discrediting of the research or the labor of Prager's monumental efforts. On the contrary, I have the utmost respect for Josh Prager: *The Echoing Green* is a riveting, amazingly detailed piece of journalistic writing, for which he deserves the gratitude not just of me, but of any serious baseball aficionado. (He was,

FOUR. Echoing Green

parenthetically, kind enough to blurb my baseball novel, *Once Upon a Fastball*, which is based on the Bobby Thomson homer.) But this has not deterred me from making the following case for what is in fact disputable and debatable about that whole sordid affair. I will, consequently, allow my pen to do its thing, to function as equalizer, scale balancer, and, ultimately, devil's advocate.

Further, as rabid as I was growing up in Brooklyn as a Giants fan, I have since, I hope, matured and, as a professional athlete and a sports student and teacher and writer, have always tried to be objective about what happens in sports in general and in particular, as difficult as this is, what occurred during that season of 1951 and on that fateful day in early October of that year.

That said, the following is the side of the debate that represents Branca's very human—emotional and perhaps myopic—reaction to the events of 10/3/51 as well as the disputability and fallacy of some of the actual scandal facts.

We know for a fact that there was cheating going on, but while we will never know for sure whether Bobby Thomson saw the sign for the fastball, the two questions that remain are 1. So what? and 2. What effect did the scandal itself have, for a full half century, on the lives of Thomson and especially Branca?

First, a few words about Bobby. Between 1951 and the end of his life (he died in 2010), he steadfastly and unhesitatingly maintained that he didn't see the sign coming from Sal Yvars in the bullpen because he was so focused on the incoming pitch. Everyone who ever knew Bobby thought that he was an exceedingly honest and humble man, so why would anyone with any objectivity and good judgment doubt his words or call him a liar?

Now for Ralph's reaction.

The segue from Bobby to Ralph—encapsulating the crux of the "he said, he said" contrast—is a quote (related in *The Echoing Green*, p. 349) by Thomson that says it all: "We did steal signs and I did take some, and I don't feel good about it. But I didn't get the sign on that pitch. Ralph says I did, and if that eases the burden of what he's carried around all these years, I'm glad for that."

As he admits repeatedly in *A Moment in Time*, Ralph Branca suffered the stigma of being the greatest goat in the history of sports for over six decades, from 10/3/51 until the very end of his life. And as devout a Catholic as he was and as much as he disliked the idea of using

Part One—Cause and Effects

excuses, that is precisely what he did when the secret of the cheating scandal was revealed in Prager's article, and later expanded extensively in his tome. As Branca states in the introduction to his memoir, after he learned about the scandal, his "tongue has certainly been loosened," and he is not afraid to complain and lament repeatedly, in the book and in his life. He even ascribed to Bobby a mental state that Bobby never admitted to, much less might have felt: "He jumped on that goddamn fastball like a tiger pouncing on some wounded antelope...." Sadly, until his last dying breath, although he did show signs of humility and forgiveness as the years passed, Branca still remained deeply bitter about "that goddamn pitch" and constantly maintained, with every fiber of his being, that at the very end when he entered the game, and only then, the game was somehow rigged, fixed, and stolen. Always the same explanation, the feeling of being cheated, never taking true responsibility for his own role in the saga of the fateful homer.

The fact is that as soon as Branca learned of the scandal, in 2001, he automatically gave himself an excuse, an out, something and someone to blame for his Disastrous Delivery. Mentally, it served as his "get-out-of-jail-free card," hearkening back to his celebrated "prison" quote: "You know, if you kill somebody, they sentence you to life. You serve twenty years and you get paroled. I've never been paroled." As a rebuttal to this, a wise quote from the ancient Chinese philosopher Lao-tzu in his *Tao Te Ching* says it all: "Failure is an opportunity./If you blame someone else,/There is no end to the blame."

Another excuse Branca used: "This homer would have been a long fly in any other ballpark." But baseball has rules and parameters, as we all know, and the Polo Grounds wasn't "any other ballpark." Woulda, coulda, shoulda....

To his credit, Branca did try to accept his fate, to move on ("I made a decision not to speak about it. I didn't want to look like I was crying over spilled milk"), to show strength, and to befriend Thomson: "I had to endure the moment in silence. I saw silence as my shield of dignity. I wanted to shout 'Fraud!' but my nature wouldn't allow it" and "It's a very hard thing to do." But ultimately, he really couldn't ever let go of the "scandal as an out" concept (the "We wuz robbed!" syndrome), of his ongoing feelings of frustration and anger. Or, as he expresses it in his memoir, "the drama of ongoing disappointment."

Sadly, I believe, this diminished his attempted courage and strength. He hated being called a whiner, but in the end, he could never overcome

FOUR. Echoing Green

his feeling of being robbed and cheated, and of being tagged for life as a loser. When the cheating scandal was exposed, he finally had something, and someone, to blame. This shortcoming, however, does cement his legacy, as least for me, as a fine human being who possessed, as we all do, the quality of human frailty and imperfection.

With respect to my—respectful—debate "rebuttal" to the Prager book, a few preliminary comments about "what ifs?"

"What if?" is, at its best, a lovely tool that can (and should) be used by creative minds. It is a rhetorical question that can be the genesis of all creative concepts, which are the sine qua nons of a significant creative product. Whether it is to create the basis for a novel or a film or a work of art or of music or even a print ad or TV commercial, it is a question that, if posed, will usually lead to a creative concept that will have considerable merit and even stand the proverbial "test of time."

But for Ralph Branca, this hypothetical question is the basis of flawed thinking that is ultimately used—albeit all too "humanly"—as a pretext for what actually happened on 10/3/51. It is also the basis of two arguments proffered by both Branca and Prager, arguments that are, for me, eminently disputable and even flawed: the fallacy of "foreknowledge," of Thomson's having seen the cheating sign, knowing what the pitch would be before it was hurled, and subsequently acting upon it; and the fallacy of the pennant playoff game being "stolen" or "rigged" (and an argument against the "efficacy of cheating").

Regarding the issue of foreknowledge, whether or not Bobby knew a fastball was coming, he still—under unfathomable pressure due to everything that was at stake between two of the bitterest rivals in the long history of sports—had to hit the ball over the left-field fence, as explained by George Plimpton (*The Echoing Green*, p. 347): "No one except the most die-hard Brooklyn fan would ever question what Thomson did.... Anyone who has watched batting practice can see how rarely even a fat pitch is hit out of the park."

Branca even agreed with this premise, saying in a *New York Times* piece, "I didn't want to diminish a legendary moment in baseball. And even if Bobby knew what was coming, he had to hit it.... Knowing the pitch doesn't always help."

Further, if Bobby indeed saw the sign and *thought* the fastball was on its way, he also knew that Branca was in control on the mound with the ball in his hand and could actually have chosen to throw the curve; or Bobby might also have been thinking, if he actually saw the stolen

Part One—Cause and Effects

signal from the bullpen, that even if catcher Rube Walker—only behind the plate because of the great Roy Campanella's injury—gave Branca the sign for the heater, Ralph could have decided independently to throw the better-advised curve, or the sign from Walker could have also been a decoy to throw off any Giants sign stealer and was actually a signal to the pitcher to go with Uncle Charlie; and.... For Bobby to consider all this would have been overthinking and, under the hugely pressurized conditions, virtually impossible.

Willard Marshall of the Giants: "When I was with the Giants we had Bill Rigney in the clubhouse with a spyglass. The funny part is that there were guys who still couldn't hit the ball even when they knew what was coming. I remember one game when we were stealing signs against Pittsburgh and they still shut us out."

Walker Cooper of the Giants: "I remember a game with the Cubs before I left the Giants. We were calling their signs from our clubhouse and they were stealing our signs from their clubhouse. And we lost, 6–0. The guys still didn't hit even when they knew what was coming."

But a lovely baseball story, told by the incomparable Willie Mays describing his facing the incomparable Satchel Paige for the first time as a seventeen-year-old, most vividly illustrates this "fallacy of foreknowledge":

> Oh, yeah. We were in Memphis, Tennessee. It was like a playoff game. It might have been '48. Satchel had a very, very good fastball. But he threw me a little breaking ball, just to see what I could do, and I hit it off the top of the fence. And I got a double. When I got to second, Satchel told the third baseman, "Let me know when that little boy comes back up." Three innings later, I go to kneel down in the on-deck circle, and I hear the third baseman say, "There he is." Satch looked at the third baseman, and then he looked at me. I walk halfway to home plate and he says, "Little boy." I say, "Yes, sir?" because Satch was much older than I am, so I was trying to show respect. He walked halfway to home plate and said, "Little boy, I'm not going to trick you. I'm going to throw you three fastballs and you're going to go sit down" and I'm saying in my mind, "I don't think so." If he threw me three of the same pitch, I'm going to hit it somewhere. He threw me two fastballs and I just swung.... I swung right through it. And the third ball he threw, and I tell people this all the time, he threw the ball and then he started walking. And he says, "Go sit down." This is while the ball was in the air. He was just a magnificent pitcher [Jason Gay, "Willie Mays Comes Home," *GQ* magazine interview, 2010].

FOUR. Echoing Green

As far as the "fallacy of stolen signs" is concerned, the flaw in the whole situation is that even if we accept the proposal that the Giants cheated (which did happen and was deplorable and disgusting) and stole the pennant from Branca and the Dodgers (*not!*), and even if Bobby knew that on the second, momentous, history- and life-changing pitch the infamous fastball was coming (which he consistently denies), the facts remain that a. stealing signs has been around a long time (two wrongs don't make a right, but...); b. Bobby has consistently claimed he didn't see the stolen sign since he was so nervous; c. if you "know" a fastball is coming doesn't mean the pitcher can't still throw a curve or a slider or a changeup; and d. most important, even if you know a fastball is coming doesn't mean you can hit it, *with everything on the line and under unspeakable pressure*, much less out of the park for a game- and series-winning homer.

And if Yvars in fact gave Bobby the sign for a fastball from the bullpen and Bobby saw it (again, he always maintained he didn't see one), a. if they suspected cheating, the Dodgers might have been giving a fake sign as a distracting tactic because logic would dictate that Branca was going to throw a curve, and b. Bobby was possibly (we will obviously never know) expecting a curve with an oh-and-one count and two runners in scoring position (he had hit a fastball off Branca for a homer in Game 1) and he was in full "swing-away mode" and wasn't in the mood, or mode, to take a called strike for an oh-and-two count, especially on a curveball. So even if he was expecting a curve, with all the adrenaline pumping, he would have been ready and focused and have reacted quickly if Branca indeed decided to toss Uncle Charlie. (After Maglie joined the Dodgers in 1956, he told his old foe and new teammate Ralph Branca, regarding the second pitch, "If you wanted him to hit the curve, why didn't you just throw him the damned curve?")

Moreover, who knows if and how much the sign-stealing system of the Giants contributed to the 37–7 winning streak at the end of the season? Here are the indisputable facts that point to stellar pitching, rather than hitting, as the major factor in the streak:

- On July 20, when the sign stealing presumably began, the Giants' team batting average was .266 at home and .252 on the road.
- From July 20 to the end of the season, the Giants' team batting average was .256 at home (or 10 points lower) and .269 on the road (or 17 points higher).

Part One—Cause and Effects

Giants' Polo Grounds clubhouse behind center field, where a telescope enabled the observation of opposing catchers' signs.

- On July 20, the Giants' pitching staff had a 3.47 ERA at home and a 4.49 ERA on the road.
- From July 20 to the end of the season, the Giants' pitching staff had a 2.90 ERA at home (or .57 points lower) and a 2.93 ERA on the road (or 1.56 points lower).

You do the math.

And why did the Giants have a spectacular road record during their season-ending winning spree, when they won fourteen of their final eighteen road games? And why did they lose, 10–0, *at home* in Game 2 of the playoffs while they were purportedly stealing signs? And why did their pitching, both at home and away, and not only their hitting play such a major role in the Giants' post–July 20 success?

FOUR. Echoing Green

A final point: in terms of the entire sign-stealing scandal and claims that the game and pennant were also "stolen" by the Giants, all this would be moot if Manager Chuck Dressen had actually made the correct call, that is, to intentionally walk Bobby and get to rookie Willie Mays, who was, as he admitted, quaking in his spikes in the on-deck circle. For one thing, Thomson had Branca's number (ironically, #13!) and had homered off Ralph in Game 1 at Ebbets Field, where the Giants had no means of stealing signs telescopically; also, that year, Bobby had already hit two homers off Branca, neither solo ones: on September 1 with one man on and on October 1 with one man on. For another, walking Bobby would have set up a potential game-ending double play or, even if Willie—much less of a home-run threat than Thomson at that point—had singled or even doubled, it would have only tied the score. And if the Giants were stealing signs, why in the world would they do so only in the bottom of the ninth, when anything could happen, and not throughout the entire game, during which they scored one measly run in the first eight innings?

Huh?

PART TWO

Agony of Defeat

Now that we have explored the various effects produced by the cause (The Pitch at the climax of the 10/3/51 game), we can move on to the underlying context behind it all. This context—the vital role that losing in sports has played and is playing in the American psyche—is the partial answer to the query "How could one fastball cause so much havoc in one man's life?" Part of the answer is obviously the incredibly high stakes at play in this one game and the pressure that accrued at its climax. But just as important was Ralph Branca's reaction to his loss, a reaction that is so typically American, a result of his competitive passion for, and pride in, winning and, in contrast, the shame and anger he must have felt in losing.

The chapters in this section of the book will explore how winning and losing are indeed impostors (a tip of the cap to Rudyard Kipling); the shame involved in losing in American sports (ditto for Jack Norworth and Boris Becker); the importance of failure in life (W.H. Auden, the concept of "ullage"); the ongoing, incessant need to win in the U.S. (our college fight songs); the relationship between hope and despair (Dante Alighieri); and, as antidotes, the lessons we can learn from ancient (Chinese, Greek, Latin) civilizations.

These considerations will hopefully shed (more) light on how the weight of Branca's loss was not only a solitary experience for him, but also how it fits into this psychological national phenomenon and profile.

FIVE

Two Impostors

*If you can meet with Triumph and Disaster
And treat those two impostors just the same....*
—Rudyard Kipling

British poet Rudyard Kipling wasn't a jock, but despite this lacuna in his résumé, he knew full well about the delusion of winning and losing. (The above quote from his poem "If" is, in fact, engraved on the wall of the Wimbledon Centre Court players' entrance, not to mention on the brains of many a high-school English student.)

Clearly, winning and losing are natural elements of life. In Lao-tzu's brilliant book of wisdom *Tao Te Ching*, we read, "Failure is an opportunity," and in Ecclesiastes 3, New King James Version, we read, "A time to gain,/And a time to lose...."

There is a season.

So why do we Americans often not accept losing? Or if so, why do we often not accept it gracefully, even with dignity?

To its credit, sports spawns strong passions, including love and hate. And hate, with maturity, transforms itself into respect. For me, this was true regarding my relationship, as a NY Giants fan from 1950 to 1957, with Jackie Robinson and Stan Musial, both of whom were thorns in the side of, and pains below the back and lower down the body for, my Jints. At the top of the list of the love/hate dichotomy is, of course, the NY Giants/Brooklyn Dodgers rivalry (you may recall the Dodgers fans' purported hatred of black and orange), and especially the 10/3/51 Game as a paradigm for many other heated rivalries: Red Sox/Yankees (baseball), Celtics/Lakers (NBA), Duke/UNC (NCAA hoops), Ryder Cup, Hogan/Snead, Palmer/Nicklaus (men's golf), Evert/Navratilova (women's tennis), U.S./Australia (men's tennis), Frazier/Ali (boxing), and Army/Navy, Lehigh/Lafayette, Ohio State/Michigan, Yale/Harvard, and, of course and especially, Williams/Amherst (NCAA football).

Part Two—Agony of Defeat

The inspirational lessons we can learn from losing are often overlooked or ignored, to our disgrace: humility, perspective, opportunity, justice, illusion, delusion, adversity, evanescence, process, unpredictability, fidelity, joy, survival....

Losing clearly tells us much more about life than winning. Which is why great fiction, art, music, and film are always about struggle, conflict, and losing.

But.

Somewhere, embedded deep in the American psyche, there is not only a burning desire to win, but also the equally burning flip side: the fear, hatred, insecurity, and shame of losing. (Think Ralph Branca.) Is it because of the hubris that comes with being the citizens of such a relatively young, feisty country? Or, because we lack the seasoning of other more mature nations, do we have slightly underdeveloped senses of irony and slightly impaired abilities to distance ourselves from the playing field and to put winning and losing in perspective? (Think Rudyard Kipling.) Or is it because we live in the land of the free and the home of the brave and have created for ourselves, over the years, the image of being winners and have placed on a pedestal a sort of immigrant, Horatio Alger, bootstraps, Little Engine That Could, *vouloir c'est pouvoir* mentality?

What's the worst invective you could possibly hurl at a fellow American? "You're a dirty bastard"? "You're a low-down, filthy, rotten, no-good, horrible, disgusting human being"? No: the lowest of the low as far as insults go might well be the disdainfully Trumpian "You're a loser!" And there's even a worse possible insult: "You're a *real* loser." It's pretty obvious that in general we Americans love, admire, align ourselves with, and root for winners; and, conversely, we shun, deprecate, would like to sew scarlet letters on, and look down upon losers. I expressed this sentiment in a poem in my collection of sports poetry, *The Heart Has Its Reasons*, titled "On Opponents":

> He brings out the best in me.
> I respect him for the same goals I aim for,
> the same qualities I honor,
> the same standards I try to maintain.
> Through hard work, courtesy, and the spirit of competition,
> he is my brother, my mirror image.
> So that when we both strive to reach a higher level,
> in unison,
> there is no loser.

FIVE. Two Impostors

Or,

That son-of-a-bitch
across the net
or on the other side of scrimmage
or guarding me
or staring at me from the mound
or lining up his putt
or moving his Queen's-side bishop
is threatening my security,
my sense of self,
my ability to succeed,
my integrity,
my pride.

God bless America.

Like most of my fellow citizens, I am proud to be an American, proud of our country's strength and resilience and courage and enthusiasm and fighting spirit. Consequently, it is not my intention to make any sweeping generalities that might appear to sound groundlessly disparaging or unpatriotic. But it seems to me that the "play-to-win-and-if-I-lose-I'm-somehow-unworthy" syndrome is particularly endemic to our fundamental national outlook and needs to be addressed. It starts at an alarmingly early age, as our young athletes are so often overexposed to this mentality by parents (generally dads) and coaches and TV networks who constantly instill the twin concepts of the thrill of victory and the agony of defeat. This excessively early start and the "win-or-go-home" training have spawned the classic quip about our country's being "East Germany with good food."

Do the names Charlie Baumann and Neil Reed ring a bell? They were the two unsuspecting students, from Clemson and Indiana, respectively, choked by two of the winningest—and most revered—coaches in American collegiate sports annals, Woody Hayes and Bobby Knight. And for every John Wooden or Tom Landry, there are probably hundreds of Vince Lombardis or George Allens or Woody Hayeses or Bobby Knights, extremely successful field generals to be sure, but ones mercilessly instilling the importance—no, *the necessity*—of winning (and, by implication, the shame of losing) to their troops.

Much has been written about greed, incivility, and violence in American sports; in my opinion, these are the natural by-products of our two national sporting instincts: the lust for winning and the shame

Part Two—Agony of Defeat

of losing. These two sides of the American coin were aptly expressed, in their most positive light, by Brit W.F. Deedes, the former *Telegraph* editor, who, writing about our 1999 Ryder Cup team, said, "I found myself feeling faintly jealous of America's capacity for emotion. We [Europeans] shrug our shoulders a lot. They really care. They want to win. They hate to lose." (If you have been following the Ryder Cup during the two decades or so since this quote, you will concede that the Europeans have indeed caught up with and even surpassed us in terms of their passion for winning, thanks in part to the passionate likes of Seve Ballesteros, Ian Poulter, Sergio Garcia, et al.)

Don't you love it when some sports announcer, witnessing a battle-to-the-death between two worthy opponents, intones, toward the end of the titanic struggle, "It's a *shame* someone has to lose"? Of course, sentimentally, I agree. But behind the ostensibly innocent broadcasting comment hides a basic disservice: the fact (of life) is that someone indeed *has to lose*. (Think Ralph Branca.) Because losing is a natural part of the fabric of sports, just as it is a natural part of the fabric of life. (Think Ralph Branca.)

Consider this: in every individual sport, where today ties have become dinosaurs, precisely 50 percent of all participants lose. Not 49 percent or 51 percent. In team sports, too, except for the 2002 All-Star baseball game debacle. In baseball, if you fail miserably 70 percent of the time as a hitter, you are still considered an unqualified success. In tennis, of the 128 participants in a major, only one player wins the tournament, and 127 "lose" it. And the odds are even worse in many golf tournaments. I'm not suggesting for one moment that we should actually attempt to lose. But for many Americans (and American coaches), *loss is not even a viable option.* And when it comes inexorably, we don't much cotton to it. Sad thing is that, like the song says, we shouldn't "care if [we] never get back" from the ball game. We should want to be there and stay there and experience sports for the sheer pleasure, joy, and passion of it.

Listen to Lou Holtz, then–assistant football coach at Ohio State: "The people of Columbus are great. They're behind you 100 percent, win or tie."

Listen to Leo Durocher, pepper-pot manager extraordinaire: "Show me a good loser in professional sports and I'll show you an idiot."

Listen to Tom Seaver, Hall of Fame pitcher: "There are only two places in this league. First place and no place."

FIVE. Two Impostors

Listen to George Brett, expert in the arts of hitting and pine-tar application: "If a tie is like kissing your sister, losing is like kissing your grandmother, with her teeth out."

Listen to Johnny Pesky, Red Sox HOFer, "When you win, you eat better, you sleep better, and your beer tasted better. And your wife looks like Gina Lollabrigida."

And listen, above all others, to Ralph Branca: "You know, if you kill somebody, they sentence you to life. You serve twenty years and you get paroled. I've never been paroled."

Winning too frequently defines who we Americans are—whether in sports, politics, personal or professional endeavors and relationships, whatever—and what we think of ourselves. There is often no place for losing in our thoughts. This thinking is so distinctly American. And at times, so distinctly alarming. An antidote to this is the importance of reflecting on the many lessons of losing that we Americans often neglect or choose not to acknowledge. True, there's nothing like winning. But equally true, despite our generally collective denial: there's nothing like losing. In fact, even though it's sometimes a bitter pill to swallow (remember: children hate to take medicine, but it's still good for them), we learn a lot more from losing than from winning. No pain, no gain. Instead of seeing losing and struggle and challenge as negatives, we Americans might do better to view them as crucibles through which we grow and learn and mature.

These are the basic underlying questions behind these lessons: What is the point of sports? Is it, as we often think, to win? Is it as simple as "winning is good, losing is bad"? Or is the goal rather to compete, to excel, to bring out the best in the human spirit? I put it this way in my 1997 volume of philosophical prose poems, *The Tao of Sports*:

> I win, you lose: so this means I'm better than you? Winning and losing are impostors, posing as self-worth and inadequacy. Do you cherish winning and detest losing? Do you think you're better or worse as a person, depending upon the result? Fact is, you're no better or worse than the fullness of your effort, than the focus and dedication and enthusiasm with which you play. If you only chase victory and fear defeat, you'll never attain balance and hold to the center. Case in point: despite his huge mound of victories, Cy Young also lost more games than any other pitcher *ever*. The Game has a way of evening things out. It is the Game, not winning the game, that will ultimately bring you satisfaction. And losing comes not from losing, but from missing out on the learning and the growth and the challenge.

Part Two—Agony of Defeat

The Olympic credo expresses the point of it all in a more eloquent and pithier way: *Citius, altius, fortius* ("Swifter, higher, stronger"). We should not, I think, translate this as meaning "swifter, higher, stronger than our opponents," but rather as "swifter, higher, stronger than what we've ever done before."

The sad fact is that, by and large, we Americans don't enjoy nearly enough the process and the struggle that sports represents. We are a nation of fierce competitors who hate to give up and love to win, yes, and that is a very good thing. But as players, coaches, and fans, we often forget to enjoy the journey and the striving, preferring to look solely at the results, the bottom line. Instead of celebrating the overcoming of obstacles and the concept of competing against a worthy opponent, we often celebrate the *W* and, conversely, end up hating, and being shamed by, the ("scarlet") *L*. We aren't generally philosophical about losing, like Boris Becker: "I lost a tennis match. It was not a war. Nobody died." Nor do we thumb our noses playfully at defeat, even when it is devastating, like French golfers Jean Van de Velde and Thomas Levet. Nor do we have a good chuckle at a closely contested but losing battle and toss back a pint (or three) of Foster's, like any true Aussie athlete. Rather, we all too often regret, lament, even cry over our losses.

On August 25, 2002, the Associated Press printed stories in my then-local Sunday paper about two of the most fiercely competitive female athletes in the world at that time. In one, Mia Hamm, arguably the greatest female soccer player ever, had just lost the WUSA championship game (her Washington Freedom were edged, 3–2, by the Carolina Courage). "We didn't come all this way to lose," Hamm said, fighting back tears. "No one is saying, 'Hurrah, we're second.'" And on the same page was a piece about the top two female tennis players. Venus Williams, talking about younger sister Serena, recalled, "She never liked losing, even when we were little.... If she didn't win, she'd cry."

And then, of course, there's Ralph Branca, on whom we can always rely regarding a quote (or three) about losing:

"I still have nightmares about that goddamn pitch."
"You have to hate losing with a vengeance."
"I've never been paroled."

All of which brings us back to nonjock Rudyard Kipling's iconic quote about Triumph and Disaster, those "two impostors." Which happens to be, but not so coincidentally, the title of a poem I wrote many

FIVE. Two Impostors

years ago about winning and losing and of course about Rudyard Kipling
and Ralph Branca and Bobby Thomson:

> A month short of his seventh birthday,
> the kid is perched in front of the twelve-inch Dumont,
> heart pounding like a Zollner piston,
> hands pressed together
> like an angel's in some Gothic altarpiece,
> but praying for a miracle of a different order.

*Clint Hartung is at third base, Whitey Lockman's at second,
the Dodgers lead, 4–2, and there's one man out for the Giants.*

> DNA and destiny have conspired to make him
> a Giants fan in Brooklyn.
> One of the Chosen,
> Israelite wandering toward hardball Canaan,
> he casts his look of faith at the black-and-white spectacle,
> makes a silent covenant with his namesake,
> and peers in for the Sign.
> (C'mon, Bobby, you can do it!)

*We're gonna stay right with it,
And we'll see how big Ralph Branca will fare
Against Bobby Thomson, and then Willie Mays to follow.*

> This poem is about hope.
> Pope's eternal-springing hope,
> only the all–American version.
> (C'mon, Bobby, you can do it!)
> Anything's possible
> in this best of all possible worlds.
> Hey! This is America,
> home of the brave,
> where dashing, daring heroes
> appear in the nick of time,
> make things right again,
> then ride off into the sunset.
> Home of Roy Rogers. Dick Tracy. Mighty Mouse.
> (C'mon, Bobby, you can do it!)

*Jim Hearn is warming up in the bullpen—he's not
appeared in relief this year. Clem Labine is throwing
in the Dodger bullpen along with Carl Erskine.
And Bobby Thomson is on the biggest spot
of his entire baseball career.*

Part Two—Agony of Defeat

This poem is about despair.
Who you kidding, kid?
This ain't the movies.
There's a sucker born every minute.
Lasciate ogni speranza voi ch'entrate, kid!
Give it up: it's oh-and-one,
and Ralph's just setting him up
for the curve low and away,
then the high, hard one.
Hey! Doncha hear the P.A. guy
announcing Series tickets at Ebbets?
Even Leo will tell you:
these nice guys'll finish second.

Bobby has never been involved in a pennant race as yet.
This is the biggest spot of his entire baseball history,
and he'll be up there swinging against big Ralph Branca.

This poem is about victory.
In thirty seconds,
at exactly 3:58 p.m.,
Bobby will circle the sacks like a seven year old,
then touch home,
and his life will change forever.
And so will yours, kid,
and you'll start believing that winning is the Grail
and that justice will prevail
and It's a Wonderful Life....

A home run will win it for the Giants and win the championship.
A single to the outfield'll more than likely tie up the ball game
and keep the inning going. So Leo Durocher comes over
to talk to Bobby....

This poem is about defeat.
In thirty seconds,
at exactly 3:58 p.m.,
Ralph will bow his head in shame,
trudge to the clubhouse,
strike the Oedipal pose of utter disconsolateness
that Barney Stein will immortalize,
and his life will change forever.
And so will the lives of lots of kids, kid,
who, tigers no more,
will lead their kitten existences,
wearing their scarlet *L*,
never daring to risk.

FIVE. Two Impostors

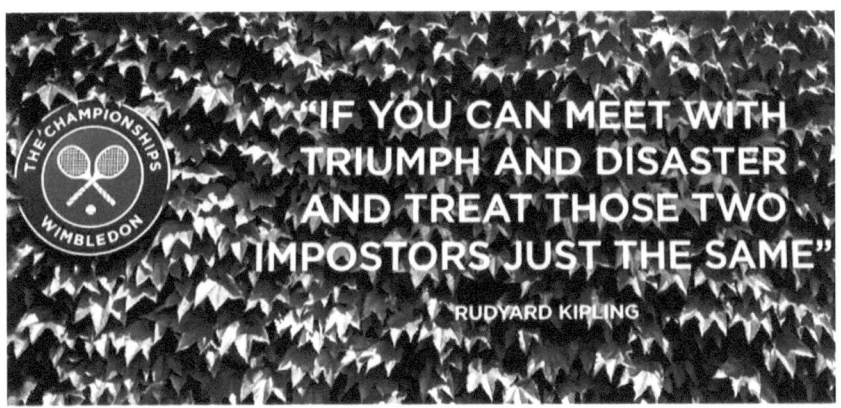

Kipling quote, engraved above the Wimbledon Centre Court players' entrance.

Branca throws ... there's a long drive....
It's gonna be ... I believe....
This poem is about striving.
Rudyard was right as rain after all:
winning and losing
are mere illusions
posing as self-worth and inadequacy.
The real hero of this saga is Ralph,
who tried his very best,
and that's all that counts,
and (as Hamlet said at the end)
the rest is silence.

Or,
perhaps he really throws the curve after all
or Bobby swings a millisecond late and pops it up
or Gil plays six inches farther to his right for Mandrake
or the wind picks up and Pafko snares it
or Sukey sends in Oisk instead
or Rube shakes off the sign
or Newk stays in
or Dressen walks Bobby to get to the rook.

Or, better still,
perhaps like Zeno's feathered dart,
that final toss never reaches its destination
and what we recall is only the striving,
the noble striving of fellow men,

55

Part Two—Agony of Defeat

the teeth-gritting, never-say-never striving
toward excellence and unfettered potential,
with no heroes, no goats,
no fame, no shame,
no strutting, no fretting,
no impostors.

The Giants win the pennant!
The Giants win the pennant!
The Giants win the pennant!
The Giants win the pennant!

SIX

It's a Shame

Let me root, root, root for the home team,
If they don't win, it's a shame....—Jack Norworth

Let's take the feeling of shame in losing in America a step further by considering this iconic pair of verses in our national baseball anthem, "Take Me Out to the Ball Game."

Despite the apparent innocence of the song in general and these verses in particular, I have always been struck by two things. On the one hand, the *L* word, not surprisingly, is avoided altogether ("If they *don't win...*"). And on the other, the double entendre ("If they don't win, *it's a shame"*) should not be disregarded: not only is it a shame (it's too bad) if they (we) don't win, but it's *a shame* (a disgrace). The sad fact is that if they don't win, many in our national midst take it to be a sign of weakness, inadequacy, or unworthiness.

So why then is *L* the American scarlet letter?

For one thing, sports losses for Americans can be crushing and leave scars, or worse. And the sport of baseball is, sadly, often a crucible that produces in both players and fans a particular loss of perspective, extreme reactions, and negative—sometime disastrous—results and lifetime scars: ostracism (Bill Buckner), vilification (Steve Bartman), hatred (Mike Torres), and even self-destruction and suicide (Donnie Moore). Not to mention, of course, "life without the possibility of parole" (Ralph Branca).

It's a *shame.*

Speaking of which, October 3, 1951, is one of the dates sometimes mentioned at the end of the historical question posed in the past to Americans: "Where were you on [date]?" Among the other frequent dates at the end of the query are December 7, 1941 (Pearl Harbor), April 12, 1945 (FDR's death), November 22, 1963 (the JFK assassination), and September 11, 2001 (9/11). Interestingly, whereas the gut reaction

Part Two—Agony of Defeat

evoked by these other four historical occurrences is shock and sadness, the feelings experienced by baseball fans to Bobby's Blast were ecstasy and pride (Giants fans) and despondency and shame (Dodgers fans, and especially Ralph Branca).

In the afterword of Bobby Thomson's memoir, *The Giants Win the Pennant! The Giants Win the Pennant!*, Branca writes:

> About that fateful pitch. I was not then, or ever, ashamed that I threw it. Disappointed? Yes. Ashamed? No. I took my best shot; so did Bobby.

Yet his exchange with Father Rowley after the game and many other passages in his memoir suggest otherwise.

I call it *loseaphobia*: instead of learning more from losing than from winning (Aeschylus had a lovely way of stating it, the concise word-pair *pathei-mathos*, or "lessons through struggle"; more on that later, in Chapter 10), American athletes tend to fear even the possibility of losing and the feeling of shame that inevitably follows. So, rather than see losing, if it does happen to happen to us, as a form of therapy or self-improvement, we often see it as something to avoid at all costs, as some form of shame or even punishment for not attaining our unwritten sporting goal (which is, of course, to win).

On the professional sports level, we see this all the time. If we think of the most competitive American athletes, those who have that intense, white-hot blaze of self-confidence and tenacity constantly flashing in their eyes, we might assume that they are motivated by one thing and one thing only: the desire to win. Now, just close your own eyes (after you have finished reading this paragraph, of course) and picture the *eyes* of some of the great competitors you can remember watching during your lifetime. I'll proffer as examples I have conjured up in my own mind the following: Babe Zaharias, Ben Hogan, Jack Nicklaus, Nancy Lopez, Dottie Pepper, Pancho Gonzalez, Jimmy Connors, Billie Jean King, Martina Navratilova, Rafa Nadal, Andy Murray, Novak Djokovic, Jackie Robinson, Bob Gibson, Pete Rose, George Brett, Jerry West, Michael Jordan, Kobe Bryant, Diana Taurasi, Nancy Lieberman, Jim Brown, Dick Butkus, Brett Favre, Gordie Howe, Alex Ovechkin, Jesse Owens, and Jackie Joyner-Kersee.

Now you can open them again. My point is this: Would it surprise you to discover that for every one of these great champions, and probably for those you have envisioned yourself, it was not only the desire to win that motivated them, but at the same time *the fear of losing*? And

SIX. It's a Shame

that these two apparently paradoxical motivations were constantly competing with each other in their various piercing gazes?

Not having earned an advanced degree in clinical psychology, I am unequipped to delve into the deeper reasons for this feeling in these athletes or the various early childhood experiences that may or may not have precipitated this particular phobia. But based on what I have read and experienced, I would venture to say that many of them, if push came to shove, would admit to being motivated partially, if not principally, by the fear or hatred of losing. Jimmy Connors has spoken of it often, as have some of the others I have listed above. But Jerry West might have expressed it best with his simple Mountaineer eloquence: "My fear of failure has been the thing that's made me get up in the morning." And this from someone who is best known as a winner, especially at crunch time.

America is, in many respects, a country made up of perfectionists. Our society is, by and large, goal-oriented and derives much of its strength—and some of its weakness—from a collective and obsessive drive to achieve and accomplish and succeed. And perfectionists, particularly in sports, have an obvious tendency to not accept anything short of total success and winning. But the opposite is true, as well: they tend to not factor in consciously as part of the competing equation the possibility of losing, which is the one factor many of them in fact fear the most. It's also common to hear these American perfectionists say something like, "I hate losing, even at ping-pong. Or Scrabble."

On the amateur level, the fear of losing is no less prevalent and taken no less seriously. Perhaps you've seen it in your own sporting ventures, or in those of your friends or children. After all, who among us actually likes that uncomfortable and sometimes humiliating feeling that accompanies losing? But why, we might ask ourselves, do we opt for fearing humiliation, as opposed to learning from humility?

The bottom line is that while our right brains should be intuitively sensing the creative and productive possibilities of the experience of losing, even our left brains should be figuring it out logically: when we fear losing (and especially when we then actually lose), we feel stressed and uncomfortable. But when we don't fear it and actually see it (if it happens, which is a reasonable percentage of the time) as the provider of lessons and of character building, then we'll feel neither stress nor discomfort, but rather peace and calm.

One of my favorite sports quotes was uttered by German tennis

Part Two—Agony of Defeat

icon Boris Becker after he was upset by a virtually unknown player: "I lost a tennis match. It was not a war. Nobody died." On top of all its philosophical profundity, it also just happens to be a tidy little poem (a sputtering quasi haiku, actually), winding down inexorably from a six-syllable statement of fact to a five-syllable metaphor to a four-syllable exquisite, ironic fusion of the two. In their staccato simplicity, these three bare-bones sentences speak volumes about winning, losing, and perspective in sports. And all this from, at the time, a freckled, baby-faced teenager who shouldn't be so wise. But how European! In fact, Boris Becker was and is unquestionably a product of European culture, of nineteenth-century Teutonic realism, of a graybeard tradition that appreciates the human condition, the philosophical perspective we Americans often lack, the greater context of the here-and-now.

I first saw Boris play in 1984, in the U.S. Open Boys' Singles draw. He wasn't quite ready then to make the main draw. Same for one of the other dominating players of the late-eighties and early-nineties, Stefan Edberg. But they both were clearly the cream of the crop, destined for greatness. You could tell by their grace, their energy, their determination, their purpose. Even then. Anyway, a few years later, in '87, two years after Boris' amazing triumph at Wimbledon at age 17, he was a heavy favorite to take that crown again, for the third straight time. Second round, he's pitted against the virtually unknown (except to the enlightened cognoscenti) Aussie, Peter Doohan (Peter *Who*-han?). So guess what happened: Boris was surprised, upset, summarily dispatched. Undoubtedly giving the delighted Doohan a yarn to spin, decades hence, to his grandchildren on some sweltering December evening Down Under. But also giving the unsuspecting reporters fits. Querying Boris after the match, eager to learn how in tarnation such an impossibility could happen, they encountered The Quote, to which, without question, there could not have possibly been a fitting response.

"Nobody died," indeed.

As opposed to the American Way, which is, quite to the contrary, dedicated to the often misguided proposition that once we enter an athletic competition, we must win at all costs. And if we're expected to win, it's particularly vital that we do. Because we *ought* to (some American drivel about a "birthright"). And this is where death comes into the picture, the very death, or its absence, to which Boris referred. For many Americans, winning and losing are for some reason not unrelated to life and death, if only in a metaphorical sense. Does it ever occur to us that

SIX. It's a Shame

losing can affect us positively? Apparently it did to Bill Bradley, ironically a "born winner," who, in his memoir *Life on the Run*, said, thoughtfully, "The taste of defeat has a richness of experience all its own." That much can be learned from the experience? That far from being the end of the world, it is in fact simply an integral part of it?

Coach George Allen—that paragon of correctitude and good living—was one of many Americans locked in a do-or-die battle with the demons of losing and death. He was purported to have once said, "Every time you win, you're reborn; when you lose, you die a little." How American! So: *Nobody died?* Well, George sure thought so. Defender of the Flag, the Pie, the Hot Dog, and, perhaps, the Chevrolet, he posited for future generations of American males the thesis that—begging to differ with Herr Becker—sports is in fact some kind of war, that it's not really about competing or excelling alone, but about winning and losing, about living (or, to use his neo–Christian allusion, *rebirth*) and dying. So what's the next logical step? That if we lose sufficiently and keep dying a little, we'll eventually end up dying *completely*, slain by the twin demons of Defeat and Shame?

Thus the lines are drawn. The European kid, Champion of Irony, is telling us it's about competition, effort, and excellence, and no big deal, nothing serious, so go out and do your best, then saunter down to your favorite Rathskeller—even with your conqueror!—and toss back a couple of Dortmunder Unions. And, on the other side of the net, the grown-up American coach, Champion of Earnestness, is telling us, quite to the contrary, that to win is to discover Resurrection and to taste defeat is to have a preliminary and premature interview with The Reaper.

Although there are obvious and numerous exceptions to both worldviews, in my experience, the rules basically prevail. A few examples on both sides will support my point.

European (French) golfer Thomas Levet, having lost to Ernie Els in a playoff for the 2002 British Open, quipped that it was "pretty good to come in second."

European (French) golfer Jean Van de Velde, after losing a seemingly insurmountable lead with one hole to play in the 1999 Open Championship before imploding, then losing in a playoff, did nothing in the days that followed but laugh off his crushing loss and say how it could happen to anyone and joke that it wasn't a life-or-death thing.

European (German) luger Georg Hackl, arguably the greatest Winter

Part Two—Agony of Defeat

Olympic champion ever, said of his competitive preparation, "I go in there thinking, well, if I lose, it's not the end of the world, then I can relax."

European (Swedish) tennis player Magnus Norman once overruled an umpire's let call on match point against him, thus awarding the victory to his shocked, but appreciative, opponent, Sebastien Grosjean, in the fourth round of the 2001 Australian Open. (Norman would no doubt have been incarcerated for such treason had he been tried in an American tennis court.)

On the other hand....

American Sam Rutigliano, ex–football coach, opined on the subject of losses, "It's like having heart attacks. You can survive them, but there's always scar tissue."

American Deacon Jones, ex–all-pro defensive end, talking about Dick Butkus, arguably the best defenseman who ever played the game, quipped, "When he hit someone, he wanted to put him in the cemetery, not the hospital."

And on the subject of the 10/3/51 game....

American Larry King, die-hard Dodgers fan, listening, at age eighteen, to Red Barber's radio broadcast of the famous Giants–Dodgers pennant playoff game, said, "I felt as if I had just died," when Bobby hit the Big One.

American Andy Pafko, Dodgers left-fielder who watched as Bobby's blast sailed over his head into the stands, mused, "Those Dodger–Giant games weren't baseball. They were civil war."

And of course American Ralph Branca, regarding the cheating scandal: "The goddamn Giants took food off our table."

We Yanks just hate to lose. (Or, as particularly proud Yank George Steinbrenner once eloquently opined, "I hate to lose. Hate, hate, hate to lose.") And for many Americans, it *seems* like a matter of life and death. The problem is, as far as the rest of the world is concerned, if we do lose, sometimes it's as if somebody *did* die! Two cases in point are the attitudes of a couple of American Olympic teams. The 1972 basketball squad, which was—admittedly—absolutely, positively, and indisputably robbed blind of the gold medal game against the Russians, took the defeat so seriously that they boycotted the awards ceremony and refused to receive their silver medals, not only then, but also at ceremonies during subsequent Olympics. And the 2000 freestyle wrestling team, unable to win a single gold medal, refused to shake hands

SIX. It's a Shame

with their opponents. Prompting coach Dan Gable to say, revealingly, "I know some people don't like us for not shaking hands. But we have freedom in America. Our reactions aren't the same as other people." Prompting German coach Wolfgang Nitschke to retort, "The Americans can't lose."

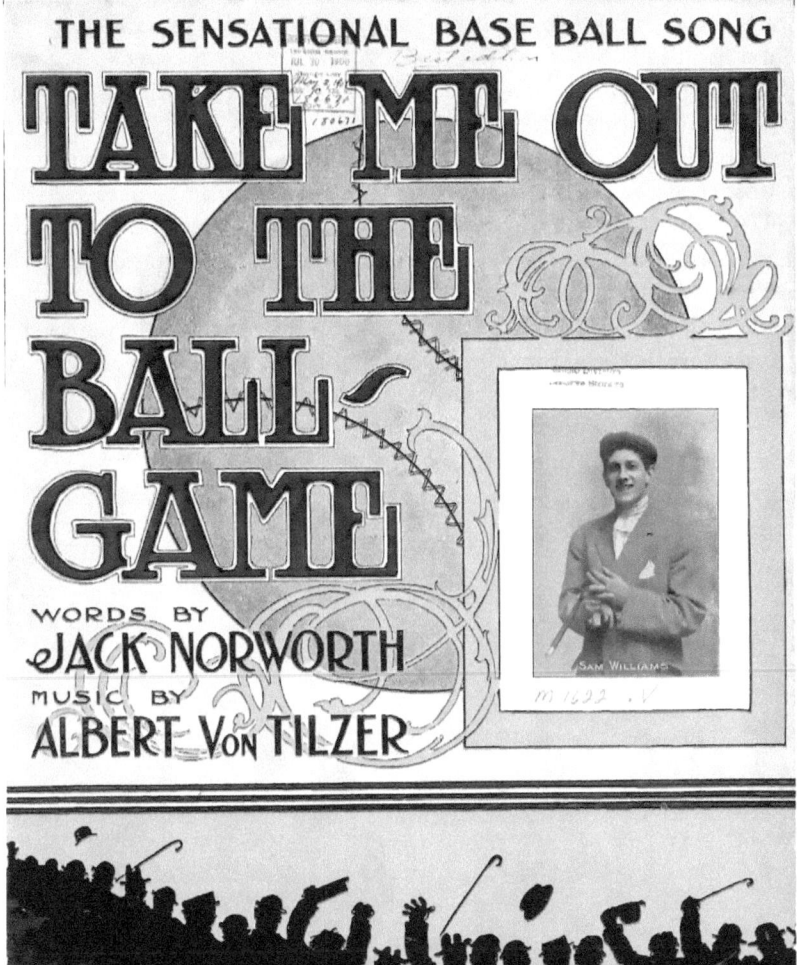

Sheet music cover of our baseball national anthem.

Part Two—Agony of Defeat

This "win-or-go-home" arrogance, this earnestness, this life-and-death attitude, this absence of humility all go a long way toward explaining why so many "foreigners" envy, resent, despise, and revile us. In an interview with Lynn Hirschberg, British actor Michael Caine amusingly explained the difference in mentalities between the Brits and us: "[we're] very good at losing. We lose everything. We lost the World Cup. We lost Wimbledon. But we do it with grace and style because we're so accustomed to it. But [we] don't like success. [The British] especially hate it if you're successful in America." And the French, begrudging the great American cyclist Lance Armstrong his brilliant accomplishment of four consecutive Tours de France, accused him—presciently, it turns out—of substance abuse. (Cries of *"Dopé!"* hounded him as he passed by the crowds.) These same French put it best—they often do—in their colloquial expression *C'est la guerre!* ("That's war!"), an alternate way of saying *C'est la vie!* ("That's life!"). The essential difference between them and us is that whereas we see life (or, in this context, sports) and war as almost literally the same, for them, the analogy is meant purely in the understated, ironic, and figurative sense.

Most tellingly perhaps, in regard to the life-and-death American attitude in sports, is one of the *New York Times* headlines the day after Bobby Thomson's three-run blast crushed the Dodgers' hopes for a chance to play in the World Series, as related by Ralph Branca in his memoir:

IT'S LIKE A WAKE IN BROOKLYN.

SEVEN

Fail Better

Ever tried. Ever failed. No matter. Try again. Fail again. Fail better.—Samuel Beckett, *Worstward Ho*

My wish is to be cremated after I die, but I often tell my wife, Susan, semi-jokingly yet actually in all seriousness, that if I were ever to be buried, I would like the epitaph on my tombstone to be "I tried!"
Full effort, not results, is everything.
To put a fine point on it, fans and athletes and coaches and parents know all too well that winning and losing are—or at least should be—the by-products of the presence or absence of a number of other factors (intense preparation, constant honing of skills, enormous effort), but beyond this, that you can't control the results of a sporting competition. In fact, "Leave it all on the field and that's the best you can do, and then let the chips fall where they may" is the common wisdom regarding winning and losing. And as we know, baseball is a game of inches and bad bounces and human error and unexpected twists and turns, so losing is always a possibility that is lurking ominously in the shadows and ready to pounce at any moment.

Except, that is, if you are trudging in from the bullpen at the end of the most important game in the glorious history of baseball between the two bitterest rivals ever with both of their millions of fans figuratively living and dying on every pitch and there's one out in the bottom of the ninth and your team is two outs away from glory but there are also two men on the team of your hated rivals in scoring position and one false move and you give up a homer and you are toast and your goose is cooked and you will have a scarlet *L* branded on your forehead for the remainder of your life.

Ralph Branca was a competitive athlete and did, we must assume, try his very best and left it all on the field in every game in which he ever pitched. But in the case of the 10/3/51 game, it turned out not to be good

Part Two—Agony of Defeat

enough for him—human being that he was—in that insanely momentous occasion. To his utter regret, Bobby Thomson parked his second fastball in the left-field stands, and for Ralph, the "Leave it all on the field and that's the best you can do, and then let the chips fall where they may" mentality must have suddenly melted away and given way to "Woe is me!" and haunted him pretty much nonstop for the duration of his existence.

As painful as it might be or sound, there is a certain importance and a practical function attached to losing and human fallibility, as well as the crucial element of learning lessons from that experience, which at best can lead to growth and freedom and at worst can lead—as it apparently did with Branca—to chronic diminishment and internal imprisonment.

What all this has to do with my passion for the acoustic guitar may have you scratching your heads, but wait. Our consciousness of our own fallibility, and its analogues *process* and *imperfection* and subsequent learning and improvement—and not necessarily the ultimate attainment of goals—is so intrinsic to the human condition. Playing the acoustic guitar (now my Martin 000-28EC and Guild DV72N) has been one of my great passions in life for over sixty years now, and yet I am still failing at it every single day. But always improving, if only incrementally. Always picking up new riffs and licks, new chord sequences, new takes on old songs. Travis-picking new rhythms and always listening to and watching the picking styles of the really great ones, without coming close to approaching anything resembling their skill levels: Les Paul, Merle Travis, Chet Atkins, Leo Kottke, Mark Knopfler, Tommy Emmanuel, Joe Robinson.... Always making the same old mistakes and plenty of new ones. Always trying my best and failing and then trying again. Or, as writer Samuel Beckett put it, "Try again. Fail again. Fail better." Always attempting to learn even small lessons from failing. Lessons that Ralph Branca appears not to have truly learned, try as he may have, from his throwing that single, tragic, traumatic fastball.

Which brings me, naturally, to the concept of ullage. I love this word, because it means absolutely nothing. Literally. Ullage refers to the empty portion of a cask or a bottle of wine or a glass. And the beauty of this concept is that you can't have full without empty, and vice versa. And without the one element, the other cannot exist. Each side can only define itself in relation to its opposite, an idea that actually goes all the

SEVEN. Fail Better

way back to Plato and his "theory of opposites" in his dialogue *Phaedo*. Every single meaningful value I have ever espoused after eight decades of living on this planet has an equally meaningful value attached to its exact opposite. I see these pairs, these dichotomies, not as positive vs. negative, as is often the perception, but as being in a very deep sense symbiotic, both contradictory and complementary. And, like the fullness and ullage in a glass, mutually inclusive, one pole dependent on the other for its very existence.

Hence, losing is one half of the competitive equation, winning the other.

Failure and losing are not simply negatives, but also equally integral parts of life and, strangely enough, necessary ones that give winning and success a context and a deeper, fuller meaning; this gift of losing is a sort of self-repechage, a "do-over" you can give yourself in order to get better. The poet Emily Dickinson said it best: "A *Wounded Deer leaps highest.*"

I have spoken previously about arrogance and humility in winning and losing, about how we Americans can be obsessed with the winning side of things and have such hatred for the "other" side. If only we could put our losses in this "ullage perspective" and take the life-and-death factor out of the equation and learn from them.

Nowhere is the "bigger picture" of learning from loss or failure more poignantly expressed than in one of my all-time favorite poems in English, *"Musée des Beaux Arts,"* written by the twentieth-century British poet W.H. Auden.

In this ekphrastic poem, Auden reflects about the issue of suffering (i.e., loss) in the context of life in general, about how it always seems to take place in the most mundane of settings, and when no one seems to be paying attention. He gives as an example a painting, Pieter Bruegel the Elder's *Landscape with the Fall of Icarus*, which takes as its subject the Greek myth in which Daedalus constructs for his son, Icarus, a pair of wings with wax feathers that will allow him to escape from the labyrinth where they are imprisoned. His admonition not to fly too close to the sun goes unheeded by Icarus, who throws caution to the wind, so to speak, and who perishes when his wings are tragically melted, sending him tumbling from the sky and drowning in the sea.

In Bruegel's painting, a ploughman is in the foreground and a ship is on the right, both going about their business and completely oblivious

Part Two—Agony of Defeat

to the tragedy that is taking place out there in the sea. (Icarus has just plunged to his death.) As Auden puts it so simply and so brilliantly:

> *In Brueghel's Icarus, for instance: how everything turns away*
> *Quite leisurely from the disaster; the ploughman may*
> *Have heard the splash, the forsaken cry,*
> *But for him it was not an important failure...*

In Bruegel's painting, but not in the poem, we also see a fisherman, close to the fallen Icarus, looking into the water, but for fish and not at the young lad; and a shepherd looking at the sky at a spot where Icarus might have been seconds ago, but not at the water, where the dying boy presently flails.

In both painting and poem, the real tragedy is not so much the death of a young man, but the fact that all the indifferent adults in his proximity who should be "paying attention" are not.

So, this death, this tragedy, for both the ploughman and the people aboard the ship, was "not an important failure." No big deal, as this odd but vital oxymoron suggests. The failure—in this case, not only the loss, but also the fatal "falling" into the sea—holds no importance for them, as they were too busy with their own agendas. What does it all matter to anyone, all this suffering and death and ... failure?

We should note that another poem, "Landscape with the Fall of Icarus," by the twentieth-century poet William Carlos Williams, consider the same reaction of indifference to Icarus' tragic end at the tragic end of his poem:

> unsignificantly
> off the coast
> there was
>
> a splash quite unnoticed
> this was
> Icarus drowning

Perhaps we Americans would do well to think about what Auden is saying (or, rather, implying) here, to look at the Bigger Picture. We lose, so what? Life goes on. Others don't really care. (In Ralph Branca's case, Dodgers fans, much of American fandom in general, and the press made him the greatest goat in sports history.) So failure is, and should be, "important" to the loser, the one who fails, as opposed to others witnessing the failure. Important in the sense that it is not the end of the

SEVEN. Fail Better

Pieter Bruegel the Elder's *Landscape with the Fall of Icarus*, c. 1555, in Oldmasters Museum, Brussels.

world (although it was literally for Icarus, but, then again, he was just a flying metaphor; and it was, figuratively and recurrently, for Branca), but instead the beginning of "failing better," as Samuel Beckett tells us, and learning from the loss. In the long run, losing often has no real significance for those of us who are *not* us. And for those of us who *are* us and who happen to lose at some point, it should have some importance, especially if we can learn from the experience and somehow be humbled by it and "fail better." Like Icarus, when we lose, who is watching us "fail"? Who, ultimately (aside from Rhett Butler, that is), really gives a damn? And unlike Icarus, who lost his life, our losses, in sports specifically, are not nearly as crucial in the grand scheme of things as we might think they are. But they do give us context.

Further, failures are the consequences of action: Icarus chose to fly too close to the sun and paid the consequences, an "important failure" for him. Likewise, Ralph threw that goddamn fastball, an action that should have been for him an important failure and a learning lesson, but try as he may (and again, he surely *did* try), he could never let go of what others thought of him and what he felt about himself, and then after the cheating scandal was revealed, he again failed to "fail better"

Part Two—Agony of Defeat

and instead made scapegoating the Giants the explanation for his own action rather than face the consequences and learn from it.

A quote purported to have been uttered, or stolen, by the American writer Jack London (whose novels *The Call of the Wild* and *White Fang* I gobbled up and adored in sixth grade) sums it up best, or at least better than I could: "Life is not always a matter of holding good cards, but sometimes, playing a poor hand well."

EIGHT

Losers Valiant

Hail! to the victors valiant
Hail! to the conqu'ring heroes....
—University of Michigan fight song

Ralph Branca's reaction to the momentous loss on 10/3/51 did not happen in a vacuum (although Hoover was president when he was growing up). The context for his anger and shame is the historical—and sometimes hysterical—attitude of Americans toward loss in athletic competition, where even admitting, or uttering, the possibility of losing is rare and winning is often the only acceptable result. And the phenomenon that is perhaps the greatest exemplar of the necessity of winning in America as a matter of warlike survival and that hardly ever contemplates the possibility of losing is, as it is so aptly named, our beloved college "fight song."

Remember the grainy old piece of footage for ABC's *Wide World of Sports* that featured that Eastern European ski jumper who crashed pathetically and painfully at the base of the jump before he even became airborne? And, accompanying it, the earnest voice-over intoning the dramatic "thrill of victory, agony of defeat" line? For me, besides being an effective piece of sentimental and dramatic visual media shtick, it has always represented a sort of polarization of the American values of winning and losing.

A simplistic polarization, I might add.

What it did was to bring—graphically and vividly—to our collective consciousness the judgments that winning is thrilling (thus, good) and losing is agonizing (thus, bad). But is it really as simple as all that? In order to answer this question, we might do well to pose some other equally important ones.

The thrill of victory, the agony of defeat: Is the reverse sometimes not true, thus putting into question the dogma that the original

Part Two—Agony of Defeat

judgments embody and also the conditioning in our national psyche that resulted in part from it? Is it not true that defeat is often thrilling in ways that have nothing to do with the adrenaline rush that comes with vanquishing an opponent? Can't it be thrilling, for instance, to wage an intense battle with a(n equally) worthy opponent and, in losing, still experience the thrill of inspiring competition? Can't it also be thrilling to learn about ourselves and about how we handle pressure and hardship and to grow in the process? And, conversely, is it not equally true that victory can be agonizing at times? What about victories marred by injury? What about hollow victories over opponents who are not worthy or have not pushed us to excel or who have brought less than their total effort to the battle? Or, as that wry coffee mug puts it: "I was hoping for a battle of wits, but you appear to be unarmed."

Aren't the images of defeat sometimes just as compelling and heroic as those of victory? Like so many rabid American sports fans, I can summon up at will the images of "victors valiant" that I have stored somewhere in the nooks and crannies of my hippocampus. Images of Bobby Thomson romping around the bases in early October of 1951 and our Olympic hockey team piling on one another in disbelief and joy in 1980 and Jimmy V running wildly and jubilantly onto the court after the Incredible NCAA Finals Upset of 1983 and the 1999 Ryder Cup team nearly mugging Justin Leonard on that seventeenth green at Brookline. But at the same time, I can also invoke many touching, inspiring, sometimes tragic and sometimes heroic images of "losers valiant" in their time of pathos: C.K. Yang embracing Rafer Johnson after losing the decathlon event at the 1960 Rome Summer Olympics and the bloodied but noble Y.A. Tittle on the sidelines against the Steelers in 1964 and the fallen Mary Decker in the 1984 LA Olympics and the losing Bosox dugout just after they blew it to the Mets in 1986 and on and on and on.

The British humorist and caricaturist Max Beerbohm once said, "There is much to be said for failure. It is more interesting than success." How George and Vince and Woody would be turning in their graves had they ever heard Max utter those foolish words! But as strange as it might sound to us, there is much truth in the statement. Indeed, losing is often more poignant and inspiring and "interesting" than winning. And there is surely more to be learned from a difficult loss than from a win of any kind. Is it by coincidence that most good art, music, and literature is built around, and finds meaning in, the conflicts, struggles, shortcomings, and failures of the human spirit and condition? (When

EIGHT. Losers Valiant

was the last time you picked up an engaging novel whose plot revolved around a totally happy person who had no worries or problems and was an unqualified success in life?)

America, lighten up!

Why do so many of us—players, fans, and coaches alike—generally regard sports as war, as winning and losing period, and the winners are the better people for it and the losers are to be pitied? We have seen it ever thus, going way back to Notre Dame coach Knute Rockne (albeit Norwegian-born) and even before him, with the fight, fight, fight until we win, win, win mentality. And then George S. Patton took it—and with it, us—to War, and we won, won, won. And then when there was no war anymore, we made our own wars, on the gridiron and the hardwood and the diamond and in the rink and on the court and in the ring. And blue-collared Rocky Marciano went undefeated and became America's darling (and before him, Joe Louis, who came back to beat Nazi Germany). And then Patton's figurative son, Vince Lombardi, taught the same lesson: winning, and nothing else, is acceptable; weakness and vulnerability are not to be tolerated. And our American Eleventh Commandment was now firmly in place: *Thou shalt not lose!* And then we saw Karl Malden in *Fear Strikes Out* push his son (Tony Perkins, playing Jimmy Piersall) to the edge with his talk of the Bosox and winning. And then we saw Pat Hingle in *Splendor in the Grass* push his son (Warren Beatty) to the edge with his talk of Yale and winning. And we understood that the good, "heroic" wars were the ones we won (Revolutionary, World War I, World War II). And the bad, "shameful" wars were the ones we couldn't win (Korea and Vietnam, and later Iraq and Afghanistan). And then Lombardi's figurative son and Patton's figurative grandson, Woody Hayes, perpetuated the obsession: victory, and nothing else, is acceptable, even if you have to mug a young man on the other team who's nearly a half-century your junior. He also—and I witnessed it personally at lunch as I sat at the table next to him in the Faculty Club when I was a French professor at Ohio State from 1974 to 1981—constantly compared football to war and even gave courses at OSU on the subject. And no wonder so many Americans are obsessed with winning, in sports and in war and in politics and in business and in relationships.

One song I recall from my halcyon days and that typified this aggressive, masculine, warlike American attitude vis-à-vis sports was written in 1941 by Hugh Martin and Ralph Blane for the musical *Best Foot Forward*. (The film was choreographed by Gene Kelly.)

Part Two—Agony of Defeat

Appropriately, this fight song—"Buckle Down, Winsocki"—was sung by the students at Winsocki Military Academy. It is possible that Ralph Branca, who was 15 when the musical made its debut on the Broadway stage (and 17 when, in 1943, it was made into a film), had actually listened to the song; it might also—educated guess—have stirred within him his competitive juices and his love of winning. The comically (now, not so much then) martial lyrics:

> Buckle down, Winsocki, buckle down
> You can win, Winsocki, if you knuckle down
> If you break their necks, if you make them wrecks
> You can break the hex, so buckle down
>
> Make 'em yell, Winsocki, make 'em yell
> You can win, Winsocki, if you give 'em hell
> If you don't give in, take it on the chin
> You are bound to win, if you only buckle down
>
> If you fight you'll chuckle at defeat
> If you fight your luck'll not retreat
>
> Knuckle down, Winsocki, knuckle down
> You can win, Winsocki, if you buckle down
> If you mow them down, if you go to town
> You can wear the crown, if you only buckle down.

And then we have, in the same vein but even at times more ferocious, the (real, not fictitious) red-blooded American college fight songs.

I remember back in fifth grade, as we whippersnappers sat and watched in the auditorium while the screen was filled with the lyrics—typed sloppily and at times faintly, no doubt on an old Smith-Corona or Underwood with a worn-out ribbon—of one college fight song after another, which we dutifully sang: Wisconsin, Notre Dame, Michigan, Yale.... And we students parroted the lyrics, while the concepts of "fight" and "win" and "victory" and "conquer" and all those other martial expressions infiltrated our innocent, impressionable American noggins.

Why did they inculcate these feelings in us through these archaic, scarily military, and frequently risible lyrics? Perhaps it was that we pre–baby boomers were being handed the American baton of achievement, success, cutthroat competition, and victory at all costs? Was this the legacy of our elders that would protect us from the slings and arrows of the outrageous, tough world outside? And now it is more than seven decades later, and I still smile that wry smile and ask those same

EIGHT. Losers Valiant

questions about the basic function of these songs in our society. Because as outdated and odd as many of these fight songs seem, they are still to this day sung and even revered at many of our institutions of higher learning by countless hordes of college and university jocks and alumni athletic supporters.

One more thing: I also remember back then asking myself why those fight songs never hailed the "losers valiant." Understand that I was a fiercely competitive athlete and person then, but that thought still occurred to me, and I wondered why I never saw anything in those lyrics about the team that competed valiantly and were brave and determined in their "fight" ... but *lost*. And I still think about that now.

Fight songs are a really good place to start in order to point out how earnest, competitive, spirited, and feisty we Americans are (and Ralph Branca was), but at the same time, how deadly serious about winning and how oblivious we often are to the possibilities of losing. In fact, I would venture to say that the clear majority of "foreigners" listening to these lyrics would view them as absolutely mindless, arrogant, and, alas, typically American.

Actually, I had lots of fun researching them on the Internet. I particularly enjoyed encountering, for the first time, such memorable beauts as "I'm so glad I go to TSU!/I'm so glad I go to TSU!/I'm so glad I go to TSU!/Singing Glory Hallelujah, I'm so glad!" (Tennessee State); "We're up to snuff, we never bluff, we're game for any fuss./No other gang of college men dare meet us in a muss" (Utah); "I'm a Sooner born/And a Sooner bred,/And when I die/I'll be Sooner dead" (Oklahoma; similar lyrics appear in the songs of Rhode Island and Richmond); "To Win, to win,/You'd like like Hell to win./But you'll have to wait/'Til the moon turns green,/And the Brass Band plays 'God Shave the Dean'!/Hi-lo, Hi-lee,/It's plain as A-B-C,/If anyone's going to win today,/It's we, we, we!" (Johns Hopkins); and my all-time fave, a song in which the word "Rah" appears as 47 percent of the lyrics (16 of 34 words): "Ring out Ahoya with an M.U. Rah Rah,/M.U. Rah Rah, M.U. Rah Rah Rah Rah Rah/Ring out Ahoya with an M.U. Rah Rah,/M.U. Rah Rah for Old Marquette. Rah! Rah! Rah!" (Marquette).

My research turned up the following breathtaking but not surprising results: of the 367 songs that came up on my laptop screen (the list didn't include every single school; I was especially disappointed not to see the fight song—if there *is* an official one—for the University of California, Santa Cruz Banana Slugs), exactly 80 percent, or 295, have some

Part Two—Agony of Defeat

reference to winning (e.g., "win" or "beat" or "victory" or "triumph"). Conversely, only 20 percent do not; and of those 20 percent, or 72 songs, a mere 18 belong to "major colleges" (Arkansas, BC, Clemson, Florida, Georgia, Indiana, Iowa State, Kansas, Marquette, Minnesota, Tennessee, Oklahoma, Oregon State, Penn, Utah, Wake Forest, West Virginia, and Wyoming).

One song, Central Connecticut State's, not only mentions winning, but sings of it as the only option: "We're starting out for victory today/ We're going to win because there's no other way." Many songs chant not only of winning, but of doing it in the most ferocious ways imaginable—crashing, bashing, and smashing through the line, and, in one case (Georgia Tech), doing something unimaginably hideous: "We'll drop our battle axe on Georgia's head, CHOP!" And in five songs, there is a mention of not simply winning, but of—despite the fact that it is one of the clear no-nos, in addition to sandbagging and not trying, in the competitive arena—running up the score, thus intentionally embarrassing the opponent. (These songs belong to Colorado and those other four football powerhouses, Bates, Jacksonville, McNeese State, and Vermont.)

Even more significant, I discovered that of the 367 fight songs, a startling and pathetic four (or 1 percent) mention "lose" or "defeat" (for the loser).

Four!

As in "Take Me Out to the Ball Game," in fight songs, the *L* word is, nearly across the board, a sort of taboo, not to be mentioned by redblooded, fighting Yankee warriors. Of the four brave schools that dare to mention anything but win, win, win, we have, receiving honorable mentions, Catholic University ("Whether we win or whether we lose, we'll never give up the fight"), University of Nebraska–Omaha ("We will cheer so all our fans will know,/Be it win, lose, or draw/Everyone for Omaha/We will fight for UNO!"), and Worcester State ("Win or lose, we keep shining bright"). You will notice that the *L* word is not naked, but rather always joined by the word *win*.

But the Grand Prize goes to an astonishingly brave, candid, against-the-grain, and definitely self-deprecatingly un–American fight song belonging to one of the most respected small liberal-arts colleges in the land, Swarthmore. Its fight song ends in a wonderfully lugubrious anthem acknowledging the very real possibility—*horrors!*—of actually losing:

EIGHT. Losers Valiant

> Though dark defeat may haunt our team,
> With vict'ry far away;
> Though Fate may work against us,
> And make the day seem gray;
> Though the standard of our enemies
> May conquer old Swarthmore;
> 'Tis then we will rise and praise thee,
> As we did in days of yore.

When I first sang these lyrics to myself, I felt—as I am fairly certain you just did, too—a tear form in the corner of my eye, not so much for the "dark defeat" looming over the Swarthmorian footballers, but for the sad state of American college sports, where only one small voice has the courage to confront, unabashedly and candidly, the inexorable specter of defeat. But my incipient tear soon desiccated and gave way to joy, as I realized that, at long last, I had indeed found a college fight song that honors and hails the "losers valiant."

It is only fitting that Ralph Branca bookend this chapter on losing valiantly and fight songs. Although he did attempt to regard his loss "valiantly" (with strength and determination), he could never quite achieve that, of course. As for the fight song of his alma mater? Ralph attended NYU, albeit for one year prior to his pro baseball career, and played baseball and basketball for the Violets. Curiously, their fight song begins with these quaint and curiously worded verses:

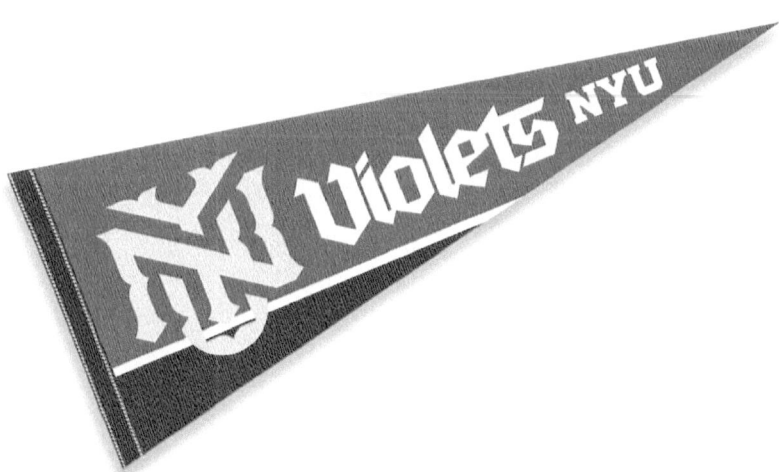

Pennant of NYU, where Ralph Branca attended college for one year.

Part Two—Agony of Defeat

Old New York University,
Drives away all adversity....

A convenient rhyme perhaps—the inappropriate options for the lyricist were *diversity* and *perversity*—but consistent with the strong tendency of college fight songs to euphemize and avoid the actual mention of "losing in battle." It was perhaps then a fitting fight song for undergraduate Ralph, seeing that he was constantly attempting (ultimately unsuccessfully) to extirpate the memory of his stinging defeat from his life, to "drive away" his shame and anger and misery that resulted from that one "goddamn pitch" and the "adversity" that it caused him personally for the rest of his life.

NINE

Hope Abandoned

Lasciate ogni speranza, voi ch'entrate.
—Dante Alighieri, *Inferno*, Canto III

"Abandon all hope, ye who enter," indeed. This inscription on the Gate of Hell, as described near the beginning of the first of three volumes of Dante's unthinkably gorgeous poetic masterpiece, *La Divina Commedia*, leaves no doubt whatsoever that sinners of all stripes who are entering the underworld can expect a one-way ticket to Hades.

As it happens, Ralph Branca described the decade that followed his infamous fastball as "absolute hell." I am fairly certain that when he uttered this metaphorical hyperbole, he was not alluding to Dante's inscription; but, judging by what he had to go through for all those years, the literary analogy does have some merit. I am also pretty sure that Ralph was not aware that the terms *absolute* (which he used) and *absolve* both derive from the Latin verb *absolvere*, to forgive or free from blame or guilt, which action he sought from his God and which he believed had been afforded to him following the news of the Giants cheating scandal.

But circling back for a moment to the discussion of ullage, the optimism/pessimism dichotomy is one of the most remarkable examples of ullage in the human spirit, the two attitudes somehow coexisting and alternating in all our lives. *Hope and despair.*

As this dichotomy relates to the Dodgers and Giants of October 1951 and to Ralph Branca in particular, we should explore the roles hope and despair (or "abandoned hope," to use a Dantean term) played in this complicated and fascinating baseball drama.

On the one hand, hope played a major role leading up to, and during, the deciding third game of the 1951 NL playoff series. As it has, in the human spirit, since time immemorial.

From Pandora's box (you will remember that after releasing all the

Part Two—Agony of Defeat

evils into the world, she closes it before Elpis, or Hope, can escape) to the Latin polymath Cicero (*Dum spiro spero,* or "As long as I breathe I hope") to the poet Alexander Pope ("Hope springs eternal in the human breast") to Russian novelist Fyodor Dostoevsky ("To live without hope is to cease to live") to NC State Wolfpack basketball coach Jimmy Valvano ("Don't give up, don't ever give up"), hope has long been one of the most inspiring of human concepts.

The most poignant illustration of the power of hope might well be O. Henry's short story "The Last Leaf," the tale of Johnsy, the deathly sick young woman who has lost her desire to live as, one by one, the leaves of an ivy vine outside her bedroom window fall. In her misery, she is determined to die as soon as the last leaf falls, but in the nick of time, her life is saved when just before his own death, a neighbor, Old Behrman, a failed artist all his life, paints an ivy leaf on the outside of her window. It is the masterpiece he had always wanted to achieve.

For me personally, and against all odds, my first glimpse of the power of hope occurred on October 3, 1951, when as a NY Giants fanatic, I witnessed on TV Bobby's blast off Ralph's high-and-tight fastball as it soared over Andy Pafko's head and just barely into the left-field stands. And hope has carried me through many of my life challenges ever since, culminating in my surviving a twelve-hour heart-and-kidney transplant surgery on July 27, 2015.

One of the great things about hope is that it can serve as the antidote to, or even a panacea for, isolation, depression, despair, fear, and doubt. (One of our great American poets, Emily Dickinson, described it as "the thing with feathers" that "perches in the soul.")

As competitive professional athletes, the Giants never gave up hope during the entire 1951 season as they chased, ran down, tied, and then ultimately defeated the hated Dodgers. And of course their devoted and rabid fans never did either, as attested, if memory serves, by yours truly. Specifically, during that bottom-of-the-ninth, last-ditch rally, even behind by three runs with only three remaining outs at their disposal, they/we always clung to the hope that they/we would find a way to prevail. For one thing, they/we had singles hitters Dark and Mueller due up to set the proverbial table for power hitters Irvin, Lockman, and Thomson. For another, as incredibly well as Don Newcombe was pitching, it was evident to many that he was tiring, so the hope was always that he and the Bums would pay the ultimate price of his mounting fatigue.

As competitive professional athletes, the Dodgers, too, never gave

NINE. Hope Abandoned

up hope during the entire 1951 season as they continued to dominate the NL field throughout the campaign, including the always-trailing Giants, especially when they held a thirteen-and-a-half-game lead in August and then held a presumably unbeatable 4–1 lead in bottom of ninth on 10/3/51, and then even 4–2, but only two outs away from victory. Just two more outs, two stinking outs, and then hope would transform itself into eternal bliss.

As a competitive professional athlete, Ralph Branca also espoused hope not only before the game began (he told us in his memoir that despite his understandable nerves, he was singing "Oh, What a Beautiful Mornin'" from *Oklahoma* at the top of his lungs during his shower that morning), but also when he came in to relieve the tiring Newk. *Only two outs away!*

Hope springs eternal.

Now all Ralph has to do is get two men out, so let's talk hope and strategy, and what might have been going through Branca's mind, or at least what he should have been thinking about, as he trudged toward the mound:

- You gotta pitch *carefully* to Bobby. Remember, he already hit a dinger off you in Game 1. No fastballs (his forte), just breaking balls!
- Walk Bobby if need be. Then, the bases will be loaded but with DP potential and nervous rookie Willie Mays up, who poses less much of a threat than Bobby does.
- If you walk Bobby and then even Willie, you'll still be up, 4–3, and you'll only have to face substitute catcher Ray Noble (a .234 hitter with only five homers) and then a pinch-hitter for Larry Jansen, who pitched well in the ninth inning and would not then be eligible to pitch in the tenth, if it comes to that.
- There is every reason to hope that you will be able to get the side out with at most one run scoring!

So that's all Ralph has to do.

"Branca throws.... There's a long drive ... it's gonna be, I believe.... The Giants win the pennant! The Giants win the pennant! The Giants win the pennant! The Giants win the pennant!"

On the other hand: *Lasciate ogni speranza, voi ch'entrate.*

And at this very moment, Pandora leaves her box open, allowing Elpis—Hope—to escape and hope is not as natural as breathing and

Part Two—Agony of Defeat

Profile of Dante Alighieri, with a quote from *Inferno*, Canto III.

Hope is not springing eternal and to live without hope is what you're feeling and "don't ever give up" is a meaningless thought.

Accompanying the feeling of hopelessness, in the mind of Ralph Theodore Joseph Branca then and thereafter, must have been the equally powerful feelings of loss and of shame and of disappointment and of anger and of letting down all that was meaningful to him in his life: he let down his teammates, his ball club, his community of Brooklyn, his Italian heritage, his God, and, finally and most disappointingly, himself. As he so poignantly stated in *A Moment in Time*, people in general placed all the blame on him, and him alone, when they concluded (my italics), "*Branca* lost the pennant."

In many people's lives, there is one traumatic event suffered at the

NINE. Hope Abandoned

outset—the death of a family member or a close friend, a serious health issue, a historical event—that, at least temporarily, dashes their hopes for a bright future. But ... *the choice of throwing a fastball?*

In the Emily Dickinson "Hope" poem mentioned above, the lesser-known second stanza is oddly prescient (unbeknownst to Emily) of the Branca situation:

> And sweetest—in the Gale—is heard—
> And sore must be the storm—
> That could abash the little Bird
> That kept so many warm—

"And sore must be the storm": the fastball Branca tossed was certainly the sorest "Gale" or "storm" he could ever imagine. Sadly, the little bird of Hope had disappeared from the scene, no longer "keeping him warm" with its "sweetest" song. Instead, the storm of that fateful pitch to Bobby Thomson ended up "abashing" Ralph's hope.

A final poetic irony: the word *abash* here means "shame."

TEN

Ancient Wisdom

*Not all storms come to disrupt your life.
Some come to clear your path.* —Paulo Coelho

The agony of defeat needn't be permanent. Or for that matter, as in Ralph Branca's case, it needn't last for over six decades. The best place to look for the antidote to this potentially crippling psychological baseball malady is probably the wisdom of the past, of writers and philosophers from revered ancient civilizations (Chinese, Greek, Latin), thinkers who viewed failure not as a negative entity (how un–American!), but rather as an opportunity to improve and to learn, a useful tool that—oddly and paradoxically—can lead to healing and even peace of mind. Lessons we could all learn from, out of the minds and mouths of our antique predecessors.

Lessons Ralph Branca might have employed, had he been aware of them, to allay his (albeit very human) senses of loss, shame, regret, anger, and injustice.

The two most prominent ancient Chinese philosophers were arguably contemporaries Lao-tzu and Confucius, the founders of Taoism and Confucianism, respectively.

In his beautiful book of wisdom, *Tao Te Ching*, Lao-tzu lays out the road to self-awareness in a series of 81 carefully crafted little nuggets of poetic wisdom. Regarding failure and the insignificance of results, two pieces of advice stand out: "Failure is an opportunity./If you blame someone else,/there is no end to the blame" (take responsibility; no scapegoating!) and "Do your work, then step back./The only path to serenity" (effort, not results, is what counts).

The writings of Confucius, in *The Analects* and other opera, contribute the following jewels of sagacity regarding human nature: "A man is great not because he hasn't failed; a man is great because failure hasn't stopped him" (persistence matters!), "Watch till the clouds part

TEN. Ancient Wisdom

to see the moonlight" (patience!), and, mirroring Lao-tzu's "if you blame someone else...," "In the archer there is a resemblance to the mature person. When he misses the mark, he turns and seeks the reason for his failure in himself" (the importance of introspection; certainly after his fastball "arrow" missed the mark high and tight to Bobby, Ralph might have looked inside himself to seek the reason for his "failure" instead of blaming the Polo Grounds' dimensions and, subsequently, the Giants cheating scandal).

Of the many philosophers, oracles, and writers in ancient Greece, the Delphic oracle—also known as the Pythia, the high priestess and oracle of the Temple of Apollo at Delphi—pronounced the two "golden rules" that reduce, with wisdom and concision, all of human experience to four spare words: *Meden agan. Gnothi seauton*, "Nothing in excess. Know thyself" (no obsessing over your losses! and look in the mirror for answers!).

Aristotle—Greek philosopher, polymath, and student of Plato—believed that learning resulted from intimately felt experience, in the mellifluent linguistic pairing *pathein ... mathein* (learn from the inside, from suffering!).

Similarly, Aeschylus, the "father of Greek tragedy," in his *Agamemnon* (176–78), expressed the sentiment of *pathei-mathos*, or "lessons through suffering," the law Zeus gifted to mortals (in sports, the lesson is to show resilience: no pain, no gain!). It's worth noting here that the English word *passion* comes from the Greek verb *pathein*, to suffer or to endure, suggesting that what is felt deeply—in love or art or any other human activity—can bear fruit only through struggle.

Menander, Greek dramatist and author of 108 comedies, put it this way: *Lupes iatros estin anthropos logos*, "For man, knowledge is the physician of grief" (the truth will set you free!).

Among ancient Roman thinkers, two of the most prominent were both known as Stoic philosophers. Marcus Aurelius, also a Roman emperor, once opined, *Haec tibi potestas est in mente, non in rebus externis. Consilium hoc, et invenies vim*, "You have power over your mind—not outside events. Realize this, and you will find strength" (or, to quote the American thinker and philosopher, Ralph Waldo Emerson, "Nothing can bring you peace but yourself"). Lucius Annaeus Seneca (Seneca the Younger), statesman and dramatist, is said to have said, *Errare humanum est, sed perseverare diabolicum*, "To err is human, but to persist is diabolical" (you're only human, so after you screw up, move on!).

Part Two—Agony of Defeat

Then there are the many wise and well-known Latin aphorisms, among which the most appropriate here are *Facta non verba*, "Deeds not words" (actions speak louder...) and *Quod nocet saepe docet*, "What harms often teaches" (listen to what Aristotle and Aeschylus are telling you!).

And if for some reason, all this profound wisdom from the distant past is not sufficient to allay the angst that plagued Ralph Branca his whole life, we should, maybe and rather, not have to look beyond the great borough of Brooklyn, the hallowed place that Branca called his baseball home for a decade (1944–1953). There, on the Belt Parkway as you are leaving Brooklyn and approaching the Verrazano-Narrows Bridge, there stands a simple blue-and-green sign that says it all, compressing the ultimate advice to be offered, to Branca and to us all, in the face of the crushing Agony of Defeat into a single, powerful, and eloquent word:

"Exiting Brooklyn" sign on the Belt Parkway.

Part Three

The Human Side

This section of the book explores the human side of Ralph Branca. How he handled the challenges of personal flaws, injustice, bad luck, conflict, heartbreak, and scapegoating. How he felt the natural needs for recognition, fair play, a lucky break, resolution, honesty, and exoneration. And in doing so, how he proved himself to be, above all, a sentient, decent, emotional, flawed, introspective, and vulnerable human being. A human being who was (as we all are, intrinsically) conflicted and complex. A mortal—as his memoir, *A Moment in Time*, also reflects throughout—who possessed all manner of traits, both positive and negative: sincerity, honesty, integrity, passion, resilience, but also anger, regret, obsession, vindictiveness, and ego.

An Everyman, if you will.

ELEVEN

Everyman

Attention, attention must finally be paid to such a person.
—Arthur Miller

I'm not all that crazy about labels, but if you pressed a pistol against my temple, I'd call myself an Emersonian transcendentalist, a fervent believer in the concepts of personal intuition, inner strength, and self-reliance.

Every once in a while, however and admittedly, we all need a little "attention to be paid," some form of acknowledgment from others: a pat on the back, a wink of approval, a kind word, or some outward sign confirming to us that we are worthy and that we are contributing, even in some minuscule and unobtrusive way, to the happiness of others and to making the world a better place.

This is why the quote from Arthur Miller's brilliant play *Death of a Salesman* is so brilliant. But before I consider the entire citation and illustrate in more personal detail why this is so, I feel compelled to mention two other quotes that are also dear to my heart, as corroborating evidence of the human need to be acknowledged and as appropriate analogues to Miller's.

The first is uttered by Clarence, the guardian angel of George Bailey, the unforgettable protagonist—played unforgettably by James Stewart—in Frank Capra's iconic film *It's a Wonderful Life*:

> Strange, isn't it? Each man's life touches so many other lives. When he isn't around, he leaves an awful hole, doesn't he?

The essence of the film, as you will recall, ultimately revolves around George's reasons for attempting to take his own life based on his financial woes and personal feelings of inadequacy and absence of fulfillment. The turning point is when George tells Clarence, after jumping off the bridge in a botched suicide attempt, "I wish I'd never been born,"

Part Three—The Human Side

and, ironically, he gets his wish granted by the angel. As George suffers through scene after subsequent scene in which (because he had never been born, in accordance with his assertion to Clarence), he goes unrecognized by all the characters he actually knew and loved and who were an integral part of his flawed life, he learns the lesson—talk about cautionary tales!—of being careful what you wish for and comes to appreciate the universal truth that, indeed, attention must be paid.

The second corroborating quote is from W.H. Auden's ekphrastic poem "Musée des Beaux Arts," which you will remember from Chapter 7 and which also considers the issue of "attention not being paid."

All of which, inexorably, leads us back to the resonant words of Arthur Miller. In the opening act of *Death of a Salesman*, Linda Loman sadly says of her defeated, delusional husband, protagonist Willie:

> I don't say he's a great man. Willy Loman never made a lot of money. His name was never in the paper. He's not the finest character that ever lived. But he's a human being, and a terrible thing is happening to him. So attention must be paid. He's not to be allowed to fall in his grave like an old dog. Attention, attention must finally be paid to such a person.

For me, this quote resonates deeply on a personal level, which is precisely the universal effect all great literature, not to mention great art and music, as well, should create inside of us. It resonates, because it points out in such a powerful way the crucial redundancy within all of us: we are both human ("he's a human being") and flawed ("he's not the finest character that ever lived"). We all have in common the *hamartia*, the "tragic flaw," of the classical Greek-tragedy protagonists, the same shortcoming or frailty in our natures as first defined by Aristotle in his *Poetics*, which was written over 2,350 years ago.

In the Miller quote, Linda could just as well have been talking, anachronistically and unknowingly, about the *hamartia* or tragic flaw of one particular baseball protagonist who, like Aristotle's tragic heroes but unlike Willy Loman, was important, capable, and powerful in his field (double entendre intended) and who had accomplished much but whose career and reputation were tragically blighted by a single blunder and who has consequently been cursed for all eternity with the humiliating epithet of *goat* (ironically, the opposite of the acronym *GOAT*). And to whom (like Willy Loman), precisely because he is a flawed human being, *attention must be paid*. Sadly, for the American baseball fan and for society as a whole, this attention is generally not paid to

ELEVEN. Everyman

a poor creature such as this because we possess the cruel tendency of sometimes not being able to forgive human frailty despite the fact that we are all genetically wired to fail with some frequency, and sometimes on the "big stage." In fact, it is this very tendency that is responsible for the pejorative moniker *goat* in the first place.

The baseball protagonist in question is, of course, Ralph Theodore Joseph Branca, an "old dog" in the metaphorical, Millerian sense, to whom attention must most definitely be paid.

There are, of course, many notable blunders in MLB history—chief among which are Fred Merkle's 1908 boner, Mickey Owen's 1941 passed ball, Bill Buckner's between-the-legs misplay of Mookie Wilson's 1986 World Series grounder, Lonnie Smith's base-running mess in 1991, and Alex Gonzalez's 2003 error—but none belonging to a player of the Aristotelian tragic-hero caliber of Ralph Branca: a noble man with a tragic flaw who commits an "error in action."

The real "tragedy" surrounding Ralph was that in the end, he was identified, and will always be remembered, by his catastrophic gaffe in the final 1951 NL playoff game; and, sadly, sufficient attention was probably not and will never be paid to him during his lifetime and beyond (he passed away in 2016).

In fact and to the contrary—and attention must be paid to this!—Branca was more than just an average pitcher during his shortish career: he had a won–lost record (88–68) twenty wins above .500; had a respectable 3.79 ERA and 829 Ks; was a three-time All-Star (1947–49); was the starting pitcher in Game 1 of the 1947 World Series and in Game 1 of the 1951 NL playoffs; and in his best year (1947) won 21 games at the age of 21 (was 21–12), sported an ERA of 2.67 in 280 innings pitched, and was second in the NL in wins, innings pitched, and strikeouts.

But.

In that fateful Game 3 of the 1951 NL pennant playoffs, he just happened to choose to throw a fastball up and in on his second pitch to Bobby Thomson, another better-than-average player whose stature and posterity were elevated—just as Branca's were diminished—by that single delivery, and the rest is Baseball History.

Regarding the comparison between "old dogs" Willy Loman and Ralph Branca, they were both, first and foremost, human beings, decent human beings in fact, who possessed human flaws and faced human challenges and by dint of being human richly deserved to have attention paid to them.

Part Three—The Human Side

There were certainly obvious differences between the two men: as opposed to Ralph, Willy, at the time of his business and family crises, was aging and time had caught up with him; he engaged in fantasies about his popularity, fame, and success (and those of his sons); he was living his life outside of reality; and he made a few attempts at suicide.

But the two also shared some important qualities that played a part in rendering them particularly human: they both harbored feelings of regret, pent-up anger, an urge to blame, self-doubt, moments of self-destruction, obsessive feelings of disappointment and failure, and a need to cope inside themselves with outside forces that cast a shadow over their lives.

Like most people, Ralph Branca was a decent and good human being; but being human, he was also a flawed, fallible, complicated one. He was not a totally good person or a totally bad person, but simply just a person. A passionate person (his Italian heritage attests to this) full of sound and fury, signifying something. In the end, his life experiences reflect what we all experience, the good and the bad, the joys and the frustrations. He made excuses and rationalized, yes, but he was also an honest and proud man. Because of what happened on 10/3/51, the one defining day of the

Original theater poster, Arthur Miller's *Death of a Salesman*.

ELEVEN. Everyman

rest of his life, Ralph Branca could at times be angry, frustrated, resentful, vindictive, and defeated. But he could, at the same time, be proud, strong, honest, patient, and forgiving. He was an admixture of conflict and contradiction. As are we all.

In essence, Ralph Branca was Everyman.

A case in point is a passage on the final page of *A Moment in Time*, in which he expresses his conflicting feelings of inner strength and vindictiveness:

> To be honest, on this final page, in spite of my abiding Catholic faith, I had planned to be true to the vindictive *paisan* within me and conclude with this thought: *In 1951, the Giants didn't win the pennant; the Giants stole the pennant.*

On pages 3–4 of the introduction to his memoir, Branca speaks ardently—and humanly—about what he would like his legacy to be, how he would (and would not) like to be remembered, and the positive (and not derogatory) attention he deserves to be paid, presumably by future generations:

> It pains me to be remembered for one unfortunate pitch—and, unfairly, a pitch surreptitiously signaled to the hitter—as opposed to a hurler who, for a number of years, had good stuff.

And in the afterword to Bobby Thomson's memoir, *The Giants Win the Pennant! The Giants Win the Pennant!*, Ralph quotes The Bard of Avon and refers to himself in the third person in order to express his sadness at the thought that his entire legacy will be a disaster while referring hyperbolically, and by analogy, to his fateful pitch to Bobby Thomson as an example of "the evil that men do": "I'm far from a Shakespeare buff, but I remembered reading a quotation from *Julius Caesar*. 'The evil that men do lives after them, the good is oft interred with their bones.' So be it with Caesar; so be it with Branca."

> *He's not to be allowed to fall in his grave like an old dog.*
> *Attention, attention must finally be paid to such a person.*

TWELVE

Big Noise

There is a justice, but we do not always see it. Discreet, smiling, it is there, at one side, a little behind injustice, which makes a big noise.—Jules Renard

What do the seventeenth word of the preamble to the U.S. Constitution and the twenty-ninth word of our Pledge of Allegiance have in common? This is obviously a softball question, but to save you valuable Google time, the answer: they are both *justice* ("in Order to ... establish *Justice*" and "with liberty and *justice* for all," respectively; my italics). Aside from the word *liberty*, this is the only word these two august texts have in common (not counting *to, the, of, and, for,* and *United States of America*). But, as many of our dads used to tell us during our challenging formative years, life often tends to be *un*just. And all too frequently, alas, so does baseball.

Just ask Ralph Branca.

The notion of injustice—as defined in Merriam-Webster's, the OED, Collins, and elsewhere—invariably includes the ancillary concepts of unfairness, the violation of human rights, entitlement, undeserved hurt/pain, grievance, complaint ("We wuz robbed," attributed to manager Joe Jacobs after his fighter, Max Schmeling, had unquestionably outboxed Jack Sharkey but saw his heavyweight title awarded to the latter), and inequality (as opposed to what happens when equality and "justice for all" prevails, which is, of course, counter to the very concept of competitive sports).

The concept of injustice, it seems to me, is also odd because it means the absence of justice (again, ullage), which may not exist in the first place. Is life intrinsically unjust? Do we inevitably suffer, as Shakespeare put it, "the slings and arrows of outrageous fortune"? Sometimes it seems that way, since we are much more sensitive when justice, a man-made construct, fails us when we ourselves fail. But when we

TWELVE. Big Noise

succeed? Doesn't justice work in our favor then? Maybe it does, but then, we are much less aware of and preoccupied with it. Why should life be fair? Or unfair, for that matter? Maybe it just *is*. Maybe things just happen, period?

Our particular, American view of injustice differs from the European one, which is often flavored with irony, even cynicism, and a reflective turning inward. As Jules Renard, a 19th/20th-century French writer, opined: "There is a justice, but we do not always see it. Discreet, smiling, it is there, at one side, a little behind injustice, which makes a big noise." And again, monsieur Renard: "Contrary to what is said in the Sermon on the Mount, if you are thirsty for justice, you will always be thirsty." And from the introspective Belgian playwright and essayist Maurice Maeterlinck: "Outside man there is no justice; within him injustice cannot be."

In general, the American perspective tends to be more visceral and earnest, marked by emotion, a touch of woe-is-meism, entitlement, and, often, outrage: "When injustice becomes law, resistance becomes duty" (Thomas Jefferson); "Justice is the great interest of man on earth. It is the ligament which holds civilized beings and civilized nations together" (Daniel Webster); "Injustice anywhere is a threat to justice everywhere" (Martin Luther King, Jr.); "Each time a man ... strikes out against injustice, he sends forth a tiny ripple of hope" (Robert F. Kennedy); "It pains me to be remembered for one unfortunate pitch—and, unfairly, a pitch surreptitiously signaled to the hitter..." (Ralph Branca).

I am often astounded by how many of these latter concepts of and attitudes toward injustice obtain in so many ways within our American "wide world of sports." Because in so many ways sports does reflect the "wide world," being one of our great metaphors for existence. How often, for instance, we say, "in sports, as in life"!

Are Foul Balls Fair?

This goes without saying, but I'll say it. *In sports as in life*, we all need boundaries. Otherwise, there is lawlessness, pandemonium, and utter chaos.

Sadly, especially in the world of sports, these blessed boundaries are often a curse in disguise, because their chaos-avoiding, built-in limitations frequently bring with them the intrinsic injustice of competition.

Part Three—The Human Side

In golf, for instance, what's so fair about a *fair*way, with its harrowing, inescapable, inequitable perils (gaping divots, lurking bunkers, bald patches, daunting collars and ridges between it and the first cut of rough)? In football, what's so fair about a *fair* catch, which is, in this manliest of all contact sports, akin to waving a white flag of surrender? In basketball, what's so just about undeserved, arbitrary, and ticky-tacky fouls called by incompetent refs? In baseball, why is it called the "foul pole," since a ball that strikes it is ruled fair?

And speaking of baseball, above all, consider Exhibit A of injustice in American sports, the various and cruel foul-ball rules, which are, at best, hardly fair.

First, since the dimensions of ballparks are wildly different, a foul ball that is in play in some parks will fall innocently, and without penalty to the offensive team, into the crowd.

Second, a centimeter one way or the other can differentiate one scorching ground ball hit down the line for a double from the same scorcher hit down the line for a harmless foul ball.

Third, a fly ball hit down the line, in foul territory, to the right- or left-field corner and caught, while being "out of play" and "foul" and harmless should the fielder bobble the ball and drop it, is nonetheless capable of devastating harm, considering that any runner may advance a base after the catch, especially the runner at third, who may well advance to score (perhaps the winning run).

Are any of these foul-ball rules fair?

As if all this weren't bad enough, how ironic it is that the sport of American baseball, our beloved national pastime, evolved from "rounders," an early form of British cricket, in which sport the batsman is allowed to hit the ball behind him, since there is no "foul" zone!

A Game of Centimeters

Baseball is, of course, one of the great metaphors for life; and, like life, it can often be a cruel game of inches, even centimeters. And how often the boundary between fair and foul, fair and unfair, and success and failure can be so arbitrary and teeny! A wisp of wind, a moment of hesitation, a single degree of spin, a bad hop, the slightest discrepancy of accuracy or timing, the very mereness of a millisecond, and, like it or not, either all is lost or to the victor the spoils.

TWELVE. Big Noise

Take Billy Buckner's famous gaffe, for example. Ninety-nine percent of the time (in fact, even more than that: his fielding average was .992, or only 128 errors in 1,556 games), he surely would have laid his glove on the dirt and trapped Mookie Wilson's pathetic bleeder instead of letting it ooze through his legs. (You might recall sportscaster Hank Greenwald's quote regarding this phenomenon: "Has anyone ever satisfactorily explained why the bad hop is always the last one?") And yet, ooze it did, and instead of being remembered as a terrific all-around first baseman, Buckner will, sadly, only be remembered as the goat of the 1986 Series.

The same is true for Bobby Richardson's being at the right place at the right time to catch Willie McCovey's liner to end the 1962 World Series or Red Sox catcher Carlton Fisk's walk-off homer just staying fair—or unfair, if you were rooting for the Reds—in Game 6 of the 1975 Series.

Or, for that matter, in other sports: Doug Flutie's Hail Mary Orange Bowl pass to Gerard Phelan or Franco Harris' Immaculate Reception or the NCAA buzzer beaters by Keith Smart, Christian Laettner, and Lorenzo Charles or a soccer or hockey shot just hitting the goal post and missing being a goal by a centimeter and bouncing back into play or a potentially game-winning field goal in football doinking tragically (or mercifully) off the crossbar or a tennis shot just nicking (or missing) the line or a golf ball plugging (or not) in a bunker or crawling (or not) into a divot or barely hitting (or not) the lower limb of a tree or a ball or a puck taking a crazy bounce or a ski or a skate or a sled hitting a hidden bump or imperfection.

A mere centimeter one way or the other, up or down, right or left, in or out, in or near, fair or foul, goal or miss, playable or unplayable, out of bounds or inbounds, hit or out, point for or against, and you're the hero.

Or ... the goat.

Speaking of whom, we can now consider the injustice of where the ball off Bobby Thomson's bat landed, instantly making him the ultimate hero and Ralph Branca the ultimate goat. First (as Branca complained about occasionally), the left-field stands at the Polo Grounds were abnormally close to home plate: at the Polo Grounds in 1951, they were only 279 feet away from home plate; today, on average, the left-field stands of major-league stadiums are 331.5 feet away from the dish. Consequently, the baseball that Bobby tattooed landed, unjustly,

Part Three—The Human Side

not harmlessly in Andy Pafko's waiting glove, but rather, harmfully—to Branca and the Bums—a mere few rows back (Branca claimed in his autobiography that it cleared the wall by "about six inches") in the stands.

Furthermore, as Branca complained about occasionally, because of the trajectory of Bobby's uppercut swing added to the trajectory of Ralph's pitch, the ball traveling toward the left-field stands possessed an enormous amount of topspin and looked like it was going to sink before it reached the left-field wall, prompting Ralph to scream to himself as he watched the ball approach the stands, *"Sink, sink, sink!"*

> ...it is there, at one side, a little behind justice, which makes a big noise.

Unhappy B

Of all the wonderful verses in all the wonderful operettas by the wonderful musical team of Sir W.S. Gilbert and Sir Arthur Sullivan, four of my favorites are sung in their 1885 operetta, *The Mikado*:

> See how the Fates their gifts allot,
> For A is happy, B is not.
> Yet B is worthy, I dare say,
> Of more prosperity than A.

This is powerful. This is true. In sports, as in life, this has to do with the seemingly omnipresent vanquishing of meritocracy (later, Gilbert refers to "happy, undeserving A" and "wretched, meritorious B"), worthiness, and entitlement by the tipped scales of injustice.

It is worth noting that one of the terms used in the G&S lyrics to specify this dilemma of injustice is *prosperity*; although it is referring more to a general sense of happiness than to monetary well-being, the issue of fiduciary prosperity and injustice is, and has long been, part of the fabric of the American professional sports scene.

Yet B is worthy, I dare say. In baseball, who "deserves" (or doesn't) to be paid more, to win awards (or not), to win games (or lose them), to get inducted (or not) into the HOF? In terms of yearly salary, I am wondering how Willie Mays and Mickey Mantle, two of the greatest ballplayers in baseball history, would have reacted, for instance, regarding the original 2023 contract of shortstop Carlos Correa. Even allowing for

TWELVE. Big Noise

cost of living and inflation, there is no need to proffer anything more than the raw statistics and numbers to see the farcical injustice of it all:

- In 1955, the year after Willie Mays won the NL MVP (.345 BA, 41 HRs, 110 RBIs), he received a salary of $12,500, with no monetary raise compared to the previous season.
- In 1957, the year after Mickey Mantle achieved the Triple Crown (.353 BA, 52 HRs, 130 RBIs), he received a salary of $60,000, including a $28,000 raise compared to the previous season.
- Willie's highest annual salary during his amazing career was $165,000. The Mick's highest annual salary during his amazing career was $100,000.
- In 2023, the year after Carlos Correa hit .291 with 22 HRs and 64 RBIs, he was offered a salary of over $26M—the *M* stands for "million" and not "Mantle" or "Mays"—annually over 12 years, for a grand total of $315,000,000.

My poem "Argument against the Existence of a Supreme Being" corroborates this point:

> Someone once figured out that in a title fight,
> the journeyman heavyweight
> James "Buster" Douglas
> earned nearly twice as much *per second*
> as the immortal Lou Gehrig did
> during his most productive *year* in pinstripes.
>
> Perhaps Nietzsche was right after all.

The great George Carlin described injustice most colorfully: "The caterpillar does all the work, but the butterfly gets all the publicity."

So let's recap. According to Sir Arthur Sullivan's lyrics referring to a hypothetical being personifying the concept of injustice: *B* is not happy, *B* is worthy, and *B* is wretched and meritorious. I'm not saying that Sir Arthur was prescient, but ... what was the first, capital letter of our Ralph's surname again?

Do-Over?

One Tuesday morning in November of 1953 (at 11:11, if memory serves), during recess, I am standing on the sidewalk just outside the

Part Three—The Human Side

playground of my elementary school, PS 180, on 56th Street and 16th Avenue in Brooklyn, New York. Facing me is Michael Krumholz, my best friend and fellow mischief-making fourth-grader. We are engaged in a hot-and-heavy, fiercely competitive game of "pennyball."

This particular sport, played on Brooklyn sidewalks throughout the borough, is the simplest of athletic competitions: all you need is a sidewalk with cracks, a penny (Lincoln or Indian Head, doesn't matter), and a Spaldeen.

Here's how it works. You and your opponent choose any three consecutive cracks in a sidewalk. You station yourself behind one of the outer cracks, your opponent stations himself behind the other outer crack, and the penny is placed right in the middle of the center crack. Then, you take turns tossing the Spaldeen toward the penny in an effort to hit it. One point every time you hit the penny. First to an agreed total (usually ten or twenty-five) wins. That's it.

So there we are, Michael Krumholz and I, standing on the sidewalk and facing each other, red-faced from the intensity of the battle, our visages twisted in maniacal poses and our lips clenched from the insane preadolescent desire to vanquish and humiliate our opponent.

It is Michael's turn, and he's between a coin and a hard place. It is 24–23, favor of me, and he needs to hit the penny to tie the game and preserve his slim chances of winning. (Even if he gets a point now, I win 25–24 if I score when it's my turn.)

"Feeling the pressure, eh?" I taunt, cruelly. Michael shoots me a quick Dick Cheney snarl, unwilling to dignify my snide remark with a rejoinder.

I can feel his little mind being squished in the vice of tension. I can see the beads of sweat forming on his troubled brow. I can almost taste the Sweet Wine of Victory.

The penny he is aiming at is in his box, only two feet or so from where he is positioned, so the degree of difficulty of his chances of hitting it is about a two on a scale of one to ten.

Imaginary drum roll. Michael's eyes, focusing intently on his target, metamorphose into tiny slits. A pregnant pause of four seconds, then, at the exact instant that the end-of-recess alarm sounds, the Spaldeen leaves his hand and wends its way toward the penny. And, by no more than a hundredth of a speck ... *it misses!*

"Yay!" I shout, with unabashedly explosive joy.

Michael is crushed, but, unsurprisingly, he refuses to admit defeat.

TWELVE. Big Noise

"Hey," he whines, "the game's not over. I get another chance. You heard that alarm bell, didn't you? I got distracted, couldn't concentrate. *I deserve another chance!*"

"No do-overs!" I screech adamantly. "You had your turn, fair and square, and I won!"

"Did *not!*" Krumholz insists.

"Did *too!*" I retort maturely. "Listen, you sore loser, didn't you ever hear of integrity? My dad taught me all about it, and how you have to do what's right, even if it hurts you."

Michael's mouth opens wide, an uncomprehending look filling his startled face.

"In other words, *no do-overs!*" I repeat even more scoldingly, my face turning beet. "No second chances! You get one shot. That's the whole point!" I am passionate (and clearly self-righteous) about this, about the fact that do-overs—in pennyball, as in life—are simply not acceptable and in fact must be avoided on pain of death.

In a world where injustice didn't exist and generosity flourished, Ralph Branca would probably be granted a do-over for his devastatingly unfortunate fastball.

If only.

The Poster Boys for Injustice

Larry ... *who?* Just as Buzz Aldrin (Buzz ... *who?*) will always be remembered—or forgotten—as the man who set foot on the moon after Neil Armstrong and just as Elisha Gray (Elisha ... *who?*) will always be remembered—or forgotten—as the true inventor of the telephone in 1876 (and not—*egads!*—Alexander Graham Bell), Larry Doby has the fortunate, yet unfortunate, distinction of being the first African American to play in the American League, but only the second to play in the majors, three months after Jackie Robinson broke baseball's color barrier in 1947. Consequently, Doby's legacy will always play second fiddle to that of his legendary predecessor.

This injustice is only exacerbated, first, by the fact that not only was Doby a member of the MLB Hall of Fame, a seven-time All-Star, and one of the American League's most feared sluggers, but also—Robinson's peerless base-running skills and baseball intelligence notwithstanding—he actually posted career numbers that, aside from Robinson's .313

Part Three—The Human Side

batting average to Doby's .288, were superior to those of Jackie's: his 17 years to Robby's 11; 1,674 games to 1,416; 5,883 at-bats to 4,997; 273 home runs to 141; 1,099 RBIs to 761; and .499 slugging average to .477.

And second, Larry Doby was the object of pretty much the same deplorable racial abuse that Robinson faced but, unjustly, received none of the PR acknowledgment and fame.

Alongside the bronze bust of Doby in the MLB Injustice Hall of Fame is that of Ralph Branca. In addition to his believing that it was unfair that Bobby Thomson's drive was a homer and shouldn't have been and that it was unfair that they ended up playing in the Polo Grounds instead of Ebbets Field and that it was unfair the Giants had to cheat in order to win the game and that it was unfair he was treated so poorly by the press and the fans and that it was unfair that someone with his outstanding pitching record had to be known solely for that one pennant game and that one pitch and that it was unfair that he had to live for six decades with all of the above weighing on him, on top of all this, he especially believed that it was unfair that people often remember the hero of that game and not him, albeit the goat, as he related in *A Moment in Time*:

I have to admit I still get annoyed when I'm introduced to some guy and the first thing he says is, "Oh, yeah, Bobby Thomson."

The Pledge Redux

I pledge allegiance to the sports of the United States of America, and to the republic for which it stands, one nation under God, indivisible, with misery, injustice for all.

Blind Injustice (*not!*).

THIRTEEN

Thirteen

If you get out of this world alive, you're lucky.
—Irv Sukenik, our house painter when I was a little kid

For many people, luck—both the good and the bad kinds—definitely does exist in the form of the number 13. For some, it portends misfortune: there is, for instance, no thirteenth floor in countless buildings; and at the Last Supper, of the thirteen guests, Judas Iscariot was the thirteenth to be seated. On the other side, to wish someone luck—the equivalent of our "Break a leg!"—the French offer the charming acronym MALPT, which stands for *merde à la puissance treize*, or "shit to the thirteenth power."

On October 3, 1951, Ralph Branca wore number 13 on the back of his Brooklyn Dodgers uni. Apparently, Ralph did not suffer from triskaidekaphobia; in fact, he embraced that controversial number and wore it with not with fear, but with pride that season because he considered 13 not to be an unlucky number, but quite the opposite. In contrast, no NY Giants player between 1947 (Mort Cooper) and 1983 (Mark Davis) sported that jersey number.

On Friday the 13th (April 13, 1951), nearly six months prior to the fateful "goddamn pitch," Dem Bums and the Bronx Bombers played an exhibition game at Yankee Stadium. As luck would have it, Branca was on the mound that day. He had apparently found a black cat that had "crossed his path" in the dugout before the game. The Dodgers won that game by a whisker, 7–6.

In addition to the jersey number and the black cat, it is apparent that—from his actions and words—Branca considered himself "lucky" (in the sense of "blessed" or "fortunate") in many respects, in the same way Lou Gehrig did when he spoke those famous words in his Farewell Address at Yankee Stadium on July 4, 1939 (my italics):

Part Three—The Human Side

> Fans, for the past two weeks you have been reading about the bad break I got. Yet today I consider myself *the luckiest man* on the face of this earth.... *Sure, I'm lucky.* Who wouldn't consider it an honor to have known Jacob Ruppert? Also, the builder of baseball's greatest empire, Ed Barrow? To have spent six years with that wonderful little fellow, Miller Huggins? Then to have spent the next nine years with that outstanding leader, that smart student of psychology, the best manager in baseball today, Joe McCarthy? *Sure, I'm lucky....*

Throughout his life, Ralph Branca frequently considered himself a man who didn't need "luck"—in the deeper sense of chance or the arbitrariness of circumstance—to make him happy: he felt fortunate to come from a very large, loving Italian family (he was the fifteenth of seventeen children); he felt fortunate to be married to a loving woman, Ann Mulvey, and to have two loving daughters, Patti and Mary; he felt fortunate to have many loving nieces and nephews and grandchildren and a loving son-in-law, Bobby Valentine; he felt fortunate to have played for the Brooklyn Dodgers and to have performed for their loyal and loving fan base; he felt fortunate to have had a successful career as a pitcher (three-time All-Star, won 21 games at the age of 21, and a won–lost record of 88–68, for a respectable .564 percentage); and he felt fortunate to believe in a loving God who bestowed upon him all these earthly gifts.

So—one of many questions concerning Everyman Branca's complicated nature—why then did such a seemingly "lucky" man feel the need for luck (i.e., chance or the whims of Fate) in his life? And another one: Why then did such a devout Catholic seem to believe that sometimes God's will wasn't sufficient to explain the results of his actions? And a third: What or who then *could* explain these for him, if not God?

These questions and their possible answers can perhaps be pinpointed, and traced back, to precisely 3:58 p.m. on Wednesday, October 3, 1951.

At that exact moment, and from all he has said about it, Ralph Branca must have felt—rephrasing the highlight of Lou Gehrig's Farewell Address—like the unluckiest man on the face of this earth. It was the one time in his life when luck seemed to have deserted him and God's plans for him seemed to go awry.

It was soon thereafter and throughout his life that Bobby Thomson's hope-crushing blast elicited numerous "what-if" scenarios, "if-only" possibilities, "woulda, coulda, shoulda" options, and "chance-

THIRTEEN. Thirteen

related" questions—many of which Branca himself posed—for which the pitcher's human side seemed, understandably, to have needed answers.

What if the home-field coin-toss decision had gone the other way? (The Dodgers won the toss but somehow decided to host Game 1, allowing the Giants to host Games 2 and 3; if they had decided to host Games 2 and 3 instead, Bobby Thomson's Shot would not have been a home run at Ebbets Field in Game 3—nor, for that matter, would the game-winner he hit in Game 1 have been a homer at the Polo Grounds.)

What if slick-fielding first baseman Gil Hodges hadn't held the nonthreatening Alvin Dark close to the bag, at the start of the Giants' bottom-of-the-ninth, last-licks rally, before Don Mueller's single just past him and in that vacated hole (which otherwise would have been a double-play ball)?

What if a tiring Don Newcombe had listened to Jackie Robinson, toughed it out, and remained on the mound to pitch to Bobby?

What if Oisk hadn't thrown that curve into the dirt warming up in the bullpen and had been called by Manager Dressen (on Coach Clyde Sukeforth's recommendation), instead of Ralph, to relieve the tiring Newk and pitch to Thomson?

What if Ralph had intentionally walked Thomson (who had already homered off him to win Game 1) to get to the nervous rookie Willie Mays?

What if, after throwing a fastball strike down the pike on the first pitch, Branca had thrown a less dangerous curve as a called strike on the second pitch, leaving Bobby with a precarious oh-and-two count?

What if Thomson's drive had "sunk," like he begged it to, and ended up in Pafko's waiting mitt?

The most human reactions to setback, disappointment, and defeat are sometimes anger (in his memoir, Branca called it his "long-suppressed rage"), resentment, frustration, and, as just mentioned, the tendency to avoid personal responsibility, to ask, "Why me?" and to deflect it elsewhere: in Ralph Branca's case, to luck or chance or circumstance or (to quote Ray Kinsella from *Field of Dreams*) the "cosmic tumblers," take your pick.

In this case, something (bad) happened to happen, and—best case scenario—you do what you can do with passion and grit (Ralph did), and the chips will fall where they may (they did). Which probably evens out, with the outcome sometimes good, sometimes bad. And so, isn't "Why *not* me?" just as valid a question as "Why me?"?

Part Three—The Human Side

In short, why did this bad thing happen to happen to Ralph? Was he simply a victim of chance, of luck? Were the cosmic tumblers simply out of line? Was it Fate or Destiny, as Branca suggested in his memoir? Was it all simply random? Was it God's intent to test Ralph? Or, as he asked Father Rowley after the game, so tellingly and so poignantly, "But why me, Father? I love this game so much. Why did it have to be me?" (He retold this story frequently not only in his memoir and in the afterword of Bobby Thomson's, but also during one of his TV interviews, when he gave it extra context, "Why did it have to be me? ... I was a guy who lived cleanly.... I was always in shape.... I loved baseball and I gave it 105 percent ... why did it have to be me? ...")

So why did God choose *him*? Why did some force greater than he (destiny? injustice? luck?) choose him to be a "victim"? Why did he, of all people, become the goat? Rather than simply take responsibility for his error (which he did, but sporadically), Branca continued to pose these entirely human queries to himself during his post–10/3/51 life. Which begs the question: did not the simple, obvious, cause-and-effect explanation ("I threw a high, inside fastball, and Bobby hit it into the stands to beat me, *period*") occur to him—without reservations or qualifications—*as the only explanation per se*?

The questions posed in the preceding eleven paragraphs are, of course, either hypothetical or rhetorical, but we should now put all this into context and consider the general concept of luck and the role it played—or didn't play—in the case of Ralph Branca's pitch and his (very human) need to attribute some credible explanation to his fateful "moment in time."

The concept of luck goes way back, at least to Fortuna (hence, the word *fortune*), the Roman goddess of luck or chance. She is often depicted blindfolded—ironically, just like the traditional depiction of Justice, but without the scales—to demonstrate her commitment to arbitrariness, capriciousness, and uncertainty.

Speaking of which, we should note that according to the Catholic faith, all events in life are the results of God's will, so, essentially and consequently, there is no such thing as luck in this religion. If not, why did devout Catholic Branca not at first accept his fate as the result of God's will and not of a chance occurrence? He did try to live with it, and to struggle with his anger and frustration, until he finally found relief upon learning about the cheating scandal. No, luck had nothing to do with it, and yes, the Giants' cheating was to blame for it all and solved

THIRTEEN. Thirteen

the problem of "arbitrariness" and uncertainty and was the sole culprit according to Branca, and the sole explanation for what befell him. But never, as far as I can ascertain, did he accept it simply as part of God's will ("Why did it have to be me?"), which would have explained it all. Ralph surely felt blessed by God, but he also evidently needed to believe in a force outside of his core religious beliefs.

The questions then remain, for us as for Ralph: Is there even such an abstract concept as luck in the first place? And do good things or bad things happen to us out of the blue, for no reason whatsoever? Perhaps they do, but maybe they result, rather, from the presence or absence of other factors, like, for instance, *preparation*? Seneca the Younger defined *fortuna*, or chance, as follows: *Fortuna est quae fit cum praeparatio in occasionem incidit.* ("Luck is what happens when preparation meets opportunity.") And nearly two millennia later, Brooklyn Dodgers president and GM Branch Rickey, who signed Jackie Robinson as the first African American MLB player in 1947, pilfered—or, rather, paraphrased—the Roman's thought when he uttered, more concisely, "Luck is the residue of design." And Ralph Branca was surely "prepared" (according to him, he was physically and mentally prepared for his "moment in time"), but obviously Fortuna didn't smile on him on that dreary Wednesday afternoon.

Another Latin aphorism comes to mind in this regard: *Virtus victrix fortunae*, or "Character conquers chance." This pithy phrase especially resonates with me, not only for its message, but also because it was the motto of my high school in Brooklyn. It is certainly true that moral strength or character is often (but, obviously, not always) capable of overcoming the vagaries of chance, and it is also true that Ralph Theodore Joseph Branca had plenty of moral strength and fortitude within him. But did he have enough to conquer chance? He struggled with this very human conflict with some success and some failure during his life, as his inner fortitude and a single unforeseen and inexplicable event and its consequences fought an ongoing battle within him to determine which side would prevail.

Which brings us, finally, around to the trope discussed in the previous chapter, namely, Injustice, and how it relates to Luck and Ralph Branca.

A reasonable premise: if something that happens to someone appears to be unfair (Injustice's "big noise"), there must be an explanation for it. *God? Destiny? Injustice? Luck?* How do people, Ralph

Part Three—The Human Side

So much for superstition.

THIRTEEN. Thirteen

Branca included, explain life's mysteries—the Good, the Bad, and the Ugly—if not by myths and abstractions and belief systems that they create in their minds and hearts for themselves? *God? Destiny? Injustice? Luck?* These are all man-made, abstract concepts that are employed by humans, especially in times of trouble, to help explain what is happening and why. Their need for a higher force, wiser and stronger than they are, to help them in times of need. A shoulder to lean (or to cry) on. An explanation of life's big question marks. And for Branca, if the injustice of what happened on 10/3/51 couldn't be explained even by God, perhaps then it was just an "unlucky" break?

On the other hand, life could simply be random, and what happens to people is either "meant to be" or, maybe more plausibly, *just happens.* After all, aren't God, Destiny, Injustice, and Luck merely absolutes? And doesn't that mean that if so, belief in any or all of these would require people to give up the control of their lives to that of something else, some higher force that is always just and fair and right?

All or some of which might help to explain why, after throwing that one goddamn fastball at precisely 3:58 p.m. Eastern time on October 3, 1951, Ralph Branca needed the concept of Luck or Chance or Fortune (take your pick) to explain—as even God could not—why this single unhappy, unfair event and its consequences in his life had to happen to him, and to him alone.

At the start of the 1952 season, Ralph Branca changed his jersey number from 13 to 12.

FOURTEEN

Two Faces

For every action, there is an equal and opposite reaction.
—Isaac Newton, Third Law of Motion

"Look both ways!" is great advice from parents teaching their kids how to cross the street safely. Which brings us, naturally, to Ralph Branca.

Janus was a very special Roman god, not only because he had no equivalent in Greek mythology, but because he was always depicted with two faces looking in opposite directions. He was also the god of an unusually large number of paired entities, including transitions and dualities, entrances and exits, beginnings and endings, the past and the future, crossing places and thresholds, and gates and doorways (his name derived from *ianua*, the Latin word for "door" and also the etymological source for the month of January and the English word *janitor*, or "door keeper").

In numerous ways, Ralph Branca was the human embodiment of Janus.

Due largely to, and in the continuing aftermath of, the humongous, pressure-filled stakes and disastrous result of the 10/3/51 Giants–Dodgers showdown, he was preoccupied with—even haunted by—a recurring series of some of the most typically human psychological conflicts and dueling forces that would certainly have fallen under the auspices of the facially bifurcated Roman god.

Crime/punishment. The final section of this book (Part Four) will consider this dichotomy in much greater detail. For now and in brief, Branca considered his act (The Pitch) as unpardonable, by himself, his teammates, and Dodgers fans. So much so that he even considered it a crime, as he so touchingly and solemnly expressed it with some frequency: "You know, if you kill somebody, they sentence you to life. You serve twenty years and you get paroled. I've never been paroled." The

FOURTEEN. Two Faces

event and its consequences are constantly in apposition to each other: the committing of a mistake, then suffering for it. As mentioned in Chapter 10, Seneca the Younger is said to have said, *Errare humanum est, sed perseverare diabolicum*. Branca's error was thus not only human, but his efforts to continue to give it oxygen compounded the "original sin."

At the same time, though, this "crime" had serious consequences in Ralph's life. His self-punishment, as well as the abuse he received from the outside world (threats on his life, on his family's safety, hate mail, and the like), complemented his crime and served as a constant reminder of it. In fact, in his afterword to Bobby Thomson's memoir, he uses a revealing extended simile to describe the severity of his punishment and the extent to which he has suffered and will continue to suffer its effects:

> Not too long ago a sportswriter compared my situation to that of an alcoholic. He said, "An alcoholic is an alcoholic until the day they put him in the ground." He's probably right. In the same sense, I'm going to hear about Bobby's homer until the day they put me in the grave.

An African proverb probably expresses most eloquently this particular "cause vs. effect" conflict: "Don't look where you fall, but where you slipped."

Self-trust/self-blame. By all accounts (his teammates, himself), Branca had a strong belief in his God-given abilities and skills. Early on in his career (for instance, 21 wins at the age of 21, which at the time—and pre–Dwight Gooden in 1985—placed him second, by only a few months, to Christy Mathewson in 1901 on the list of youngest pitchers to win 20 games or more), he proved to himself that he could achieve great success as a professional baseball player, that he could consistently perform well, even in clutch situations. And his inner moral strength was never in question, either. Had he been steeped in Ralph Waldo Emerson's transcendental thought (he probably wasn't), he would have espoused the great thinker's quote from his essay titled "Self-Reliance": "Trust thyself; every heart vibrates to that iron string." And had he read Shel Silverstein's poem "The Voice" to his daughters while they were growing up (he didn't, since the poem was published in the 1996 collection, *Falling Up*, when Branca was 70), he would have shaken his head in agreement:

> There is a voice inside of you
> That whispers all day long,
> "I feel that this is right for me,
> I know that *this* is wrong."

Part Three—The Human Side

Yet.
Ralph Branca cared deeply about his legacy, about what people thought of him; and although he often needed, in retrospect, to have something or someone else to be responsible for his own actions, he also harbored much of the guilt and the shame and the blame for his single dramatic and monumental blunder. The "Why me?" syndrome, if you will. He certainly did not wish to be remembered or perceived solely as that guy who blew The Game single-handedly by throwing that fateful fastball. (The closest parallel was people remembering Bill Buckner not for his splendid baseball career, but solely for his fielding butchering of Mookie Wilson's little squibber in Game 6 of the 1986 World Series.) And in opposition to his positive self-regard, he was rankled by the thought that he was often not remembered for his own worth, but in the context of someone else (you will recall his "Oh, yeah, Bobby Thomson" quote recently cited).

Reason/emotions. Ideally, these two phenomena can coexist peacefully, as Benjamin Franklin remarked: "If passion drives you, let reason hold the reins." But they can also be at odds with each other, as they often proved to be in Ralph Branca's life.

On the one hand, in his mind, the quest to find a reason, an explanation—whether from God, a scapegoat like the Giants following the discovery of the cheating scandal, or just bad luck—for what happened in early October of 1951, and why, was recurrent, nagging, and burdensome.

On the other hand, and conflicting with the need to know and to explain, were the raw emotions Branca felt throughout his life concerning the 10/3/51 game and the traumatic repercussions of his "goddamn pitch." These deep feelings were pretty much—as he himself explains in detail in his memoir—a result of his passionate and feisty Italian heritage and temperament. (His father, John Branca, was an Italian immigrant who, in 1888, arrived in America with his family as a young child. Ralph was named after his grandfather, Raffaele.) The feelings in question were numerous and quite diverse, ranging from rage and resentment to frustration and depression to shame and regret. And, finally, vindictiveness, to which he frankly refers on the final page of his memoir and which, according to his original intention, was even more powerful and motivating than his belief in The Almighty (Ralph's italics):

In 1951, the Giants didn't win the pennant; the Giants stole the pennant.

FOURTEEN. Two Faces

In essence, for Ralph Branca, emotions often ended up clouding the quest of reason and the answers it seeks, with these reactive elements overpowering any proactive efforts aimed at resolution. But they did often serve a purpose, albeit a temporary one, that of a sense of catharsis and relief (the linguistic irony here is that Ralph appeared in The Game as a "relief" pitcher but neither enjoyed nor supplied any of that as a result of his second, disastrous pitch).

The explanation of this particular conflict, reason vs. emotions, within Branca would not be complete, however, without quoting the man himself, from the introduction of his memoir:

The drama of ongoing disappointment is central to this narrative. At some point, reason and rage clashed head-on.

Reason/faith. This dichotomy pits the two opposing forces against each other, an "action" and an "equal and opposite reaction," to use Isaac Newton's terminology. Reason and faith are two opposite sides of the same coin, which attempt to explain the meaning of what happens in life in general and, in Branca's case, what happened to him on and following October 3, 1951. Was there a logical, reasonable explanation for the "Why me?" query, or was it simply meant to be, as part of God's cosmic plan?

This dilemma has many important and appropriate literary/historical precedents, the most compelling of which was a major concern for the seventeenth-century French philosopher and mathematician Blaise Pascal in his work titled *Pensées* (*Thoughts*), which were literary "fragments" that, together, argued for the existence of God and that basically constituted a defense of Christianity. Pascal's thoughts concerning "existential anxiety"—i.e., the fear and trembling caused by chaos and the blindness of ignorance about life's meaning and purpose, and a universe without God—are expressed on a cosmic level, as opposed to Branca's, but there are revealing and significant points of contrast and comparison.

Both Pascal and Branca struggled with reason, with using rational thought to explain the meaning of life, and both rejected this concept as a solution to life's problems: Pascal's *Le coeur a ses raisons que la raison ne connaît point*, "The heart has its reasons that reason doesn't have a clue about," and Branca's *Why did it have to be me?*

Blaise and Ralph also struggled with the concept of man's ignorance. In the Frenchman's case, man's not knowing why he exists in the

Part Three—The Human Side

universe and being lost in the chaos (Why are we here on Earth, anyway? Where do we fit in the grand scheme?) produced in him a feeling of terror (he famously stated, *Le silence éternel de ces espaces infinis m'effraie*, "The eternal silence of these infinite spaces terrifies me"):

> When I see the blind and wretched state of man, when I survey the whole universe in its dumbness and man left to himself with no light, as though lost in this corner of the universe, without knowing who put him there, what he has come to do, what will become of him when he dies, incapable of knowing anything, I am moved to terror, like a man transported in his sleep to some terrifying desert island, who wakes up quite lost and with no means of escape.

For Ralph Branca, not knowing why he had to be the one who became the reviled goat and the object of ridicule and hate as a result of The Pitch terrified him, as well. Reason, like in Pascal's struggle, was not sufficient to explain this conundrum.

The solutions to this problem of ignorance that the two men produced were, however, worlds apart. In the struggle between faith and reason ("Pascal's Wager," *le pari*), Pascal finally ended up rejecting reason and found solace in faith, in the comforting existence of God. Branca, on the other hand, while rejecting reason, did believe in God as a devout Catholic but felt that even his faith in God couldn't help him find solace amid his chaos. His best solution to his ignorance was the outlet and explanation of the cheating scandal, but even that didn't give him true, lasting comfort: in the end, he could never let go of his struggle and—despite his Christian beliefs and friendship with his nemesis, Bobby Thomson—was never able to forgive the Giants hero or to accept his side of the story.

Humility/ego. The etymology of the word *humble* is *humus*, Latin for "ground." So metaphorically, humility can be defined as the quality of lowering oneself to the ground. Practically, the characteristics of a humble person generally include admitting when you're wrong, giving credit to others, admitting your foibles and flaws, putting your family and friends first, respecting others, and graciously thanking opponents, win or lose.

Two exemplars of humble people that immediately come to (my) mind—aside from modern-day figures like Mahatma Gandhi, Mother Teresa, and Nelson Mandela—are Jesus Christ and sixteenth-century French philosopher and essayist Michel de Montaigne.

FOURTEEN. Two Faces

The humility of Jesus is almost too well known to mention, but in brief: he was born in a lowly manger; lived with the poor and the downtrodden; and died, accepting his fate, on a cross.

As for Montaigne, intellectual humility is reflected in the title and content of his literary masterpiece, *Essais*. The linguistic import of his title was that his thoughts were, merely and humbly, just *essais*, or unfinished, unpolished attempts at expressing himself—the etymology of *essay* dates back to the late Latin verb *exigere*, "to ascertain or weigh," which evolved into the French *essayer*, "to try or attempt"—without the promise of fully resolved answers (following in the philosophical footsteps of Confucius and Socrates). His *Essais* (107 essays in all) is replete with themes of humility—including the questioning of beliefs, the acceptance of limitations, and the embracing of imperfections—especially in his longest essay, the skeptical and Pyrrhonist *Apologie de Raimond Sebond*, which contains the pithy statement "Que sçay-je?" ("What do I know?"), which he—brilliant man that he was—had engraved on a metal cast that he wore around his neck. This is, incidentally, the humble opposite of Charles Barkley's memoir title, *I May Be Wrong but I Doubt It*. Finally, at the very end of *Essais*, Montaigne declares, "Et au plus eslevé throne du monde, si ne sommes assis que sus nostre cul," or "And on the loftiest throne in the world, we are still only seated upon our asses."

Pardon the following (lengthy) parenthesis, but whenever I mention the name Montaigne and the concept of humility—in my writings, my conversations, or my deepest thoughts—it immediately and inevitably triggers two reactions: 1. the issue of humility in American sports (or, more appropriately, the relative absence of it); and 2. from among all the memories rattling around in my hippocampus, two in particular that took place in the late-1980s and that might contribute some useful context to the present "humility" discussion.

First....

Rare indeed are displays of being modest in victory or gracious in defeat or humble recognitions of one's limitations and fallibility, but among the few that have occurred: Jim Brown gently placing the football on the ground in the end zone after scoring one of his then-record 106 touchdowns, or Barry Sanders scoring one of his 109 TDs and calmly flipping the ball to the official in the end zone, as opposed to the celebratory histrionics of today; John Wooden's quote "Talent is God-given. Be humble. Fame is man-given. Be grateful. Conceit is

Part Three—The Human Side

self-given. Be careful."; Bill Russell—the greatest team player and winner in the history of sports and the first African American NBA head coach—not attending his own Hall of Fame ceremony because he felt that Chuck Cooper, the first African American to be drafted by an NBA team, should have been elected before him; and Vitas Gerulaitis' response when he finally beat Jimmy Connors after losing to him in sixteen straight matches: "Nobody beats Vitas Gerulaitis seventeen times in a row." On the other hand....

Examples of prideful, hubristic characters abound in Greek mythology: among many others, Oedipus, Icarus, Narcissus, and of course the hare who raced the tortoise in Aesop's famous fable. And in literature: Marlowe's Doctor Faustus, Shelley's Victor Frankenstein, Flaubert's Emma Bovary, Melville's Captain Ahab, and Fitzgerald's Jay Gatsby. But neither mythology nor literature can rival the pride, hubris, and testosteronaphilia that have long run rampant in American sports. Including: former NBA great Charles Barkley's titling his memoir *I May Be Wrong but I Doubt It*; all those imperious headshakes, taunts, showboating, victorious sneers and grimaces, arrogant dancing, chest pounding, spiking in the end zone, attention-getting putting of hand to ear to elicit (more) boisterous cheering, rubbing your nose in it, rubbing salt in the wound, sore losers, spoiled sports, excuses; Mike Tyson's cannibalistic threat to Lennox Lewis ("I want to eat his children."); Alabama's Tommy Lewis tackling Rice's Dickie Moegle from out of bounds in the 1954 Cotton Bowl; the trash talking and on-court and on-field rudeness of Connors, McEnroe, Tarango, Garnett, Rodman, Sprewell, Sherman, Woods (no, not that one: *Ickey* Woods), Cobb, Rose, et al.; and the boorish manners of coaches like Knight and Hayes.

Sadly, this entire bunch reminds me of those animals that make themselves look bigger than they are by beating their chests (apes), puffing themselves up (lizards), or fanning their tail feathers (peacocks). And to continue the wildlife motif, they also remind me of the old English proverb: "When they came to shoe the horses, the beetle stretched out his leg."

And second....

It is a freezing early morning in December of 1990, and I am waiting on the raised train platform at the Chappaqua, New York, station, where I then lived, for the 6:46 that will take me to Grand Central Station in New York City, where I worked in advertising. On the platform, I happen to bump into Bert Sugar, the late and great boxing guru.

FOURTEEN. Two Faces

Recognizing him immediately (with his funky broad-brimmed fedora and omnipresent cigar), I introduce myself as a lifelong athlete and fellow sports fanatic and engage him in superficial sports banter, which we continue to enjoy throughout the hour-or-so commute into the City.

Our chat soon devolves into some high-octane, nonstop athletic kibitzing and opining; and at one point during the train ride, we begin to toss out hot-and-heavy trivia questions right and left and at a dizzying speed. After the first few challenges, I am feeling pretty confident because I am holding my own against him despite the fact that his very advanced brain is a bottomless repository of sports flotsam and jetsam. I parry each of his potentially devastating left jabs and return them with my own potentially devastating right crosses.

"Where was Willie Mays born?" Bert asks smugly.

"Westfield, Alabama," I reply with stunning speed, grinning inside. And then I add, for good measure as the grin rises and settles in my lips and cheeks, "May 6, 1931."

"Who was behind the plate when Branca threw the gopher to Bobby?" I riposte, arching my eyebrow defiantly. *I got him good this time*, I am thinking.

Without an ounce of effort, Bert offers, "Rube Walker, 'cuz Campy was hurt," then, adds blithely, "Oh, and also behind there was ump Lou JOR-da," fastidiously enunciating the initial syllable of the surname with a playfully vicious and supercilious snarl.

Game on.

"What were Ron Sobie's and Connie Mack's real last names?" Bert queries, his upper lip quivering slightly and his dilated shark-like eyes sensing blood.

Cool as a cucumber, I respond, with peacock pride, "Sobieszczyk and McGillicuddy."

My turn. After a few seconds, I am thinking, *I've got him this time. The perfect trivia question. Yay.*

"Okay, which boxing champ had a surname that is a palindrome?"

Now, this is a devilishly tough question because it not only requires a thorough knowledge of boxing history—which Bert has in spades, and then some—but also 1. a knowledge of the meaning of the word *palindrome* (a word or phrase reading the same backward and forward; my two personal faves are "A slut nixes sex in Tulsa" and "Go hang a salami, I'm a lasagna hog") and 2. the ability to make an instantaneous nexus between word and boxer.

Part Three—The Human Side

In less than half a millisecond—I hardly get the question out when Bert nearly steps on my line—and without even blinking, as if he were camped in my brain and knows my answer, Bert retorts, guns ablazing, "Willie ... *PEP!*"

My spirit wilts under the heat of his awesome mental nimbleness and his broad, victorious grin; and, not having packed a white flag in my briefcase that I could take out and wave, all I could offer him was a hangdog look of defeat and a sheepish grin. Looks like I will be eating crow for lunch with a slice of humble pie for dessert.

But by far the greatest lesson of humility I ever learned was, ironically and fittingly, in a place of learning, a classroom. Admittedly, the following is not a story about sports, but it is one consistent with the aforementioned themes of pride and humility and learning and Montaigne and American competitiveness and testosteronaphilia.

It is November of 1988, and I have been teaching an advertising class for many years (with the late and great art director Seymon Ostilly) at the School of Visual Arts in New York City. The course, which meets one evening a week for three hours, is titled "Thinking 101," because great print ads are produced not by great writing or great artwork or great layouts or great design or typeface, but by great thinking, great concepts. The students are all trying to put together advertising portfolios to present to creative directors at ad agencies, who will hopefully be impressed by their work and hire them. The course (I state with all humility) has always been popular and has always drawn crowds.

I am giving the students an inspired and inspiring (in my mind) ten-minute minilecture about the creative process. At one point, I am speaking urgently and passionately about writing headlines and proffering my two Golden Rules (like the Delphic Oracle's), which I have attempted to drum into their heads from the very first class a few months before.

"Now don't forget, you guys: never, *ever* write a two-word headline; and second, don't *ever* try to be cute. No puns, no word plays, no pithy, coy, obtuse, quick sound bites. I promise you, these two rules will be invaluable to you as you sally forth in your advertising careers, and you can thank me later!"

A student in the back row raises her meek little hand.

"I know you've talked about this before, but can you explain again why not?"

I bite my lip and formulate the words in my head quickly but

FOURTEEN. Two Faces

carefully before responding to her. *Do my Royal, Official Pronouncements mean nothing to you? Are you not heeding my Wisdom from On High? Is it, for some inscrutable reason, not sinking in?*
Deep breath.
"Well, let me be clear," I respond arrogantly. "To write a good headline, with a strong concept, you need a little room to express an idea intelligently. You need words that are clear, direct, intelligible, and also provocative. Words that are married to your visual in a symbiotic way, so that one can't exist without the other. To achieve all this, two words—with a few exceptions, like Doyle Dane Bernbach's iconic print ad for VW, THINK SMALL—just aren't enough!"
Calm down, I am telling myself. She'll get it, maybe after the 1,548th time.

The moment is finally here, on Judgment Day. It's the part of the class when all the students present their ads from the assignment of the previous week, which was simple yet difficult: execute an ad about Bayer aspirin. Now, aspirin happens to be a "preemptive" category, or one in which there are no real differences between the brands (aspirin is aspirin), so the ad has to, in some way or another, stand out from the crowd by being provocative and memorable.

The students approach the two large walls in the classroom and attach their aspirin ads with pushpins, then take their seats. The walls are now filled to the brim with all kinds of ads that contain all manner of thinking. Seymon and I flash superior smiles at each other.

One by one and in order of their ads' positions on the wall, the students explain how they came up with their concepts and executions, hold up their ads, read their headlines, and then await our criticism and, if they're lucky, our praise. The first six students present their ads, which range from abysmal to not bad. Seymon comments on layouts, positioning, alternative visuals, media usage. I criticize language, nuance, clarity, verbosity, coyness, and whether the headline is redundant or complementary in regard to the visual.

And then, without fanfare, student #7 steps up to the plate. She is a copywriter wannabe, and the ads she has previously presented to us have shown promise but have not particularly been jaw-droppers.

She proceeds to explain her ad with sublime simplicity and directness: "This is an ad for Bayer aspirin," she begins. "I had just seen the musical *Les Misérables*, and I kept thinking about the title. So I came up with this ad. The visual is the musical's emblem, an etching of the waif

119

Part Three—The Human Side

Cosette, from Victor Hugo's novel. I changed the visual so that her right arm is raised, and I stripped into her hand a bottle of Bayer aspirin. The headline is...."

The class, Seymon, and I wait with low expectations but hopeful anticipation.

"...Less Miserable."

Talk about jaw-droppers. Mine is on the floor.

The humility of it all! The ignominy! The shame! I had drummed into these students' heads the irrefutable, written-in-stone Two Mitchell Commandments of Headline Writing, again and again, with the certainty of knowing and the presumptuousness of a true believer, and what did this rank amateur and clueless tyro present to the whole class, and in my very presence? Why, nothing less than an ad with a headline *that contains two words and is also an outrageous pun!*

And to make matters worse, the ad she presented, in my opinion, is absolutely brilliant. It seems so effortless, and yet I'm certain that she worked her butt off to come up with the concept.

And to make matters even worse than that (is this possible?), she is the very same student who asked me to repeat my two Golden Rules of Headline Writing less than an hour earlier. Was she torturing me, like in a Poe short story, knowing full well that she had created an award-winning ad that broke into smithereens my Headline Rules?

So there I am, sitting on the desk at the front of the class, my jaw still on the floor, brought down to Earth by nemesis, revenge, and retribution exacted upon me, my nose rubbed in it, the human embodiment of the expression "hoist with his own petard." Yep, cocksure, arrogant, hubris-engorged Oedipus Mitchell! I felt like nothing less than the poster boy for the John Wooden quote: "It's what you learn after you know it all that counts."

We are still only seated upon our asses.

After swallowing my considerable pride, I apologize sheepishly to the class and promise them (and myself) never again to be dogmatic and never again to prod and cajole them into following any of my brilliant, rigid rules. The great irony is that I myself am a believer that, when appropriate, the breaking of rules is one's absolute responsibility and even personal duty.

What do I know?

(Writing about all this humility has given me a bit of a headache, so I think I'll take two Bayers, feel less miserable, and call you in the morning.)

FOURTEEN. Two Faces

So where does Ralph Branca fit into the discussion of humility, and its opposite, ego, which is the personal pronoun *I* in Latin?

A devout Catholic, Ralph was, at heart and at his core, a good, decent, and, yes, humble man in his personal life. According to the general qualities of humility mentioned above, he could easily check off three of the six boxes: admit to his flaws, put family and friends first, respect others.

But at the same time—how proud Janus would be!—as good and humble a man as he seemed to be in his personal life, he could in some respects also leave blank the other three "humility boxes": admit he was wrong, give credit to others, graciously thank opponents.

Were it not for that one goddamn fastball, this would almost certainly not be the case. But the event of 10/3/51 resulted in his repeated emphasis on the persecution by himself and by others and his focus on his personal well-being. Until this pitch, it did not seem to be in Ralph's nature to be a complainer or someone who was less than humble and who put himself before others. Or someone who would ask the rhetorical question *Why me?* Or would think in terms of his own sorrowful plight (*Woe is me!*).

It is also noteworthy that in the three-page introduction to his memoir, he uses the pronoun *I* 46 times. Although it is entirely normal to use this pronoun in a book about yourself, one can't but help notice the particular plethora of this pronoun's occurrence. To be fair, most athletes (or politicians or actors or anyone in the public eye and especially at the highest levels of their fields) must by definition possess a fairly healthy ego. As did Branca, who as a professional baseball player wanted to be seen, by himself and by others, as someone who not only gave it his all, but who also believed that he excelled at what he did. But after that pennant loss against the hated Giants, he became, as reflected in his interviews and his writing, intensely concerned with *his* legacy, *his* reputation, *his* worthiness in the eyes of others, and especially being absolved of *his* "sin."

The past/the future. This was actually one of Janus' major preoccupations, as it was for Ralph. In all his visual representations (statues, paintings, drawings), Janus is seen looking to the left and the past, and at the same time looking to the right and the future. Likewise, Ralph Branca spent much of his post–10/3/51 life shuffling between reliving the past (a persistent obsession) and moving on to the future (a daunting, if not impossible, task, according to him).

Part Three—The Human Side

Statue of two-faced Roman god, Janus.

This back-and-forth from past to future is apparent throughout much of Branca's memoir; and his book ends, appropriately, with the following three sentences that reflect this past/future dialectic:

> The better part of me wants to forgive the Giants and their scheme. Forgiving them is the right thing to do. I'm trying, but it looks like it's going to take me a couple of more years to get there.

It is also notable that the title of both Ralph's memoir and the final chapter of his book is *A Moment in Time*, which not only denotes that dastardly instant in the past (precisely 3:58 p.m. on Wednesday, October 3, 1051), but also connotes the continuum of life into the future.

FIFTEEN

Pagliaccio

Ridi, Pagliaccio, sul tuo amore infranto!
Ridi del duol che t'avvelena il cor! —Canio, the clown

"Laugh, clown, at your broken love! Laugh at the pain that poisons your heart!" These words, sung by Canio, the main character in little-known Italian composer Ruggiero Leoncavallo's two-act opera, *Pagliacci* (*Clowns*), are part of arguably the best-known and most dramatic brief aria in the entire history of opera.

In short, this melodramatic opera is about a jealous clown in the acting troupe who ends up murdering his wife, Nedda (also an actor), and her lover, Silvio. In Canio's aria *"Vesti la giubba"* ("Put on the costume"), the clown expresses his pain at discovering Nedda's infidelity as he puts on his makeup for a performance. Although his heart is broken, the show must go on (*"La gente paga, e rider vuole qua,"* "The people are paying, and want to laugh here"). This, then, is the familiar theme of the tragic clown laughing on the outside but crying on the inside.

The aria also happens to reflect yet another of Ralph Branca's utterly human and Janus-like conflicts ("laughing on the outside but crying on the inside," to quote Branca himself), but one that now deserves a short but discrete separate chapter.

In fact, Ralph actually mentions the parallel between him and Canio in his memoir. During the winter following The Game, Ralph was invited by the BWAA (the Baseball Writers Association of America) to attend their dinner and "do shtick with Thomson." He agreed to this potentially mortifying experience with grace and dignity and ended up singing a bittersweet duet with Bobby, a parody of the song "Because of You," Tony Bennett's 1951 hit.

Bobby's part:

> Because of you, there's a song in my heart
> Because of you, my technique is an art

Part Three—The Human Side

Canio, in *Pagliacci*, as interpreted by the incomparable Enrico Caruso.

FIFTEEN. Pagliaccio

> Because of you, a fastball high
> Became a dinky, chinky fly
> Now Leo and me won't part
> My fame is sure, thanks to your Sunday pitch
> Up high and low, I don't know which is which
> But come next spring, keep throwing me that thing
> And I will swing, because of you.

Ralph's part (he married his fiancée, Ann Mulvey, just a few weeks after The Game; note the coincidental, unintentional, and revealing evocation of George Bailey's similar wish in the opening line!):

> Because of you, I should have never been born
> Because of you, Dodger fans are forlorn
> Because of you, they yell "Drop dead!"
> Several million want my head
> To sever forever in scorn
> One lonely bird had a word for my ear
> The only girl—what a pearl—of good cheer
> I lost the game but wound up with the dame
> She took my name ... in spite of you

In *A Moment in Time*, after citing these lyrics, Branca explains, tellingly:

> I guess I felt a little like Pagliacci [N.B. This error—this should be Pagliaccio, the singular for the clown, and not Pagliacci, the plural and the title of the opera—was caught neither by Branca nor his coauthor, David Ritz], laughing on the outside but crying on the inside. At home at night, I still had nightmares about that goddamn pitch. I couldn't wait for spring training.

The touching humanity and honesty of this quote is clear: using the stereotype of the clown (aptly chosen, since both Canio and Branca came from passionate Italian heritage), the Dodgers pitcher expresses the discomfort he felt attempting to laugh off his infamous pitch while at the same time suffering internally. And in doing so, Ralph displayed a deeply human(e) sense of good sportsmanship and grace amidst his pain and torment.

It is notable that the subtitle of his memoir is *An American Story of Baseball, Heartbreak, and Grace*. Branca's story was certainly that, and so much more.

SIXTEEN

(Scape)goat

To be called a goat—as I was—for half a century hurt like hell....—Ralph Branca

In the Old Testament book of Leviticus, the *Azazel*, or "scapegoat"—the English term was coined by Protestant scholar William Tyndale in 1530—is a particular goat sent into the wilderness (and pushed down a ravine, where it died) to bear the sins of the Israelites on Yom Kippur, the Day of Atonement. Similarly, in sports, the (scape)goat is an athlete who is, conveniently, blamed for the defeat of his or her team and who bears its "sin." This is an unfortunate occurrence for the scapegoat, but an apparently necessary and nefarious human need for the oppressor.

As it happens, scapegoating—that is, our urge to blame defeat on someone else, to supply ourselves with an external reason for our losses, and to transfer our responsibility to the "other"—seems to be a particularly natural and instinctual American trait. Which elicits the sociological/psychological query: why in fact do we Americans in particular cling to this despicable concept?

Call it what you will—scapegoating, schadenfreude, the blame game, finding a whipping boy, blaming a fall guy, handing someone a dunce cap and putting them in a corner, doling out a booby prize, rooting against the bad guy in the old TV Westerns—but there is a very long tradition of scapegoats in U.S. history, with seemingly endless exemplars, racial and otherwise, including: minorities and immigrants in general, the Salem witch trials, Jim Crow laws, the "Palmer Raids," the Red Scare, the Japanese internment camps, Sacco and Vanzetti, McCarthyim, the Rosenbergs ... and even the Thanksgiving turkey.

Scapegoats are particularly numerous in the history of American sports, and especially in our national pastime. The most egregious example of the sometimes disastrous results of scapegoating in baseball

SIXTEEN. (Scape)goat

is that of pitcher Donnie Moore: after throwing a home-run pitch to prevent his California Angels from winning their first pennant in 1986 and then being hounded by the press and booed mercilessly by the fans, he committed suicide three years later at the tender age of 35. Other players who were ostracized, hectored, humiliated, or otherwise tormented by fans and the press as scapegoats include Hack Wilson, Ernie Lombardi, Mickey Owen, Fred Merkle, and ump Don Denkinger.

Quite possibly the most persecuted scapegoats are my three *B*s: Bill Buckner, Steve Bartman, and Ralph Branca.

For decades after he allowed the Mookie Wilson squibber to ooze through his legs and into right field in the sixth game of the 1986 NLCS, Buckner was ostracized and humiliated by fans and the press and ended up moving to Idaho, never quite able to live down the shame of that horrifying "moment in time."

Chicago Cubs fan Steve Bartman was vilified for years by virtually the entire city of Chicago after, while sitting in the stands, he interfered with Cubs right fielder Moisés Alou during Game 6 of the NLCS against the visiting Florida Marlins. The painful irony of this misdeed was the very act of scapegoating by the Cubs fans, literally recalling the "Curse of the Billy Goat" of 1945, when similarly, Cubs fan Billy Sianis (and his pet goat!) were tossed out of Wrigley Field during the 1945 World Series against the Tigers (which the Northsiders eventually lost in seven games, never to return to the Series until 2016).

And third but not least, of course, is Ralph Branca ("I've never been paroled," "hurt like hell," "Oh, yeah, Bobby Thomson").

Although Branca was the most obvious choice to be the scapegoat for the press and the Dodgers fans after the Coogan's Bluff playoff loss, they had a number of other "scapegoat options." They could have chosen, for example, first baseman Gil Hodges, who mystifyingly was holding Alvin Dark (no threat to steal second under the circumstances) close to the bag in the bottom of the ninth when Don Mueller's grounder—which would have been a devastating, dispiriting, rally-killing double-play ball had Hodges been playing correctly off the base—went by him harmlessly into right field. Or they could have chosen Manager Chuck Dressen, who began to lose control of himself and his club in the bottom of the ninth: neither did he alert Hodges to play off the bag at first nor did he himself make the decision as to whom to bring in to relieve Newk after the Lockman double. Or Clyde Sukeforth, who did make that decision and should have known that Branca

Part Three—The Human Side

had already give up a dinger to Thomson in Game 1 and should have chosen Erskine to come in, or even Clem Labine. Or Don Newcombe, who, exhausted, decided to remain in the game (partly goaded into it by a stubborn Jackie Robinson) even after the two consecutive singles by Dark and Mueller. Or even "Oisk," who had the audacity to throw a curve down in the bullpen dirt while warming up, just before Dressen asked Sukeforth who was ready, and thus eliminate his relief viability and candidacy.

But Dodgers fans and the press had a way more eligible scapegoat candidate in Ralph Branca to condemn and vilify and label as a villain for life (his very name became a moniker for catastrophe) because of that one tragic—goddamn—pitch made under the most inconceivably immense amount of pressure during the most inconceivably important sporting event. Because no matter which gaffes and misjudgments led up to The Pitch, it was in fact The Pitch itself that was the prima facie evidence and the direct cause of the disastrous effect: Branca fastball up and in ... Thomson swings and connects ... *ball game.*

An ironic footnote to this tragedy's story: at precisely 3:58 p.m. Eastern time on October 3, 1951, *scapegoat* Julius Rosenberg's mind was not on his eventual execution, but on his beloved Dodgers and eventual fellow scapegoat, Branca. He was listening to the game in the Sing Sing death house; and afterward, he wrote a note to his wife, Ethel, also a Sing Sing prisoner: "Gloom of glooms, the dear Dodgers lost the pennant!"

A second ironic footnote involves the paradox of two terms, *goat* and the acronym GOAT. In one fell swoop (kudos here again to Shakespeare, in *Macbeth*, Act 4, Scene 3), the 10/3/51 game produced not only a goat (Branca), but also—for Giants fans, at least—a GOAT (Thomson). As stated in the prologue to Bobby's memoir:

> His is a story of almost fairy-tale, once-upon-a-time proportions—an immigrant youngster from Scotland who is a baseball star in his adopted land and with one swing of the bat becomes an American legend.

And again:

> Ancient Greek dramatists created a device to solve the difficulties of a wayward plot in need of a dramatic ending. The deus ex machina usually took the form of a godlike figure that would descend to the stage at a moment of near defeat and achieve, with a mighty blow, battlefield success. Though a mere mortal, Bobby Thomson became the Giants' deus ex machina for one glorious day.

SIXTEEN. *(Scape)goat*

The "scapegoat" ritual of Yom Kippur.

Further, although the baseball player GOAT is clearly, in my opinion, Willie Mays, the 10/3/51 pennant playoff game is the baseball game GOAT. One pitch, one homer, and Giants fans now had someone in GOAT Bobby Thomson to enshrine as a hero for life (his very name became a moniker for triumph), someone more than a pretty

Part Three—The Human Side

good journeyman player, because of one swing of the bat made under the most inconceivably huge amount of pressure during the most inconceivably important sporting event.

A third ironic twist is that scapegoat Ralph Branca felt, at different times, that he needed one in order to not be one himself. Consequently, he blamed the Thomson homer on the dimensions of the Polo Grounds ("It was a good pitch. It was a cheap home run..."), and then a few years after the cheating scandal first broke, he blamed the loss on the Giants.

And yet a fourth bit of irony: Bobby could very easily have been the goat and not the GOAT—on three separate occasions!—had he not connected in the bottom of the ninth off Branca. In the second inning, he smacked an apparent double to left, but Lockman, who was on first, held up at second because of left-fielder Andy Pafko's strong arm, but Bobby didn't (instead, he ran, head down, into a tag by Robinson). In the bottom of the eighth, when the Dodgers scored three times to take the lead, 4–1, Bobby could have prevented two of those runs had he not committed fielding misplays on grounders by both Pafko and Cox. But the roles weren't reversed: Bobby wasn't the goat, and Ralph was, as one of the next-day newspaper headlines pithily trumpeted:

THOMSON THE HERO, BRANCA THE GOAT.

In all fairness, the scapegoating of Ralph Branca for what occurred on 10/3/51, and understanding what he had to endure for half a century and the burden that the schadenfreude of others placed on him, are perhaps the most cogent arguments for feeling sympathy, empathy, and compassion toward this basically good and humble human being. As scapegoat, his punishment by his tormentors (the fans, the press, and himself) surely didn't fit his crime....

PART FOUR

Crimes and Punishments

Ralph Branca's "crime" of throwing that one fastball was obviously metaphorical. But his infinitely greater punishment was indeed, to him, intensely real: "You know, if you kill somebody, they sentence you to life. You serve twenty years and you get paroled. I've never been paroled." So he was in effect equating, albeit figuratively, his tossing that fatal gopher ball to committing a murder.

In this final section of the book, Branca's crime and punishment will be considered in the context of, and in comparison with, seven others, selected from some of the great works of world literature. These iconic literary works are truly international in scope and have been plucked from multifarious cultural sources: Biblical (Old Testament), Greek (Aristotle's *Poetics* and Sophocles' *Oedipus Rex*), American (Nathaniel Hawthorne's *The Scarlet Letter*), Russian (Fyodor Dostoevsky's *Crime and Punishment*), German (Franz Kafka's *The Trial*), and French (Albert Camus' *The Myth of Sisyphus*). And they feature a diverse cast of unforgettable characters (Adam and Job, Oedipus, Hester Prynne, Rodion Romanovich Raskolnikov, Josef K., and Sisyphus).

These crime-and-punishment comparisons might at first blush appear to be hyperbolic, but Branca's "story" has certain literary qualities—including metaphorical/symbolic value—and many commonalities with some of the great stories and characters in literary history. All compared and contrasted with, and hopefully contextualizing and illuminating, arguably the most egregious baseball crime ever perpetrated: that one goddamn fastball, thrown premeditatively and with malice aforethought, by Ralph Theodore Joseph Branca.

The revelatory questions that will be posed during these comparative analyses: What were the crimes (theft, disobedience, judgment, adultery, murder, none at all)? What were the punishments (expulsion, plague, disfigurement, shunning, imprisonment, torture)? Were they exacted internally (inside the "criminal") or externally (by God, by gods,

Part Four—Crimes and Punishments

by laws and society)? Did they fit the crimes or were they unjust? Were they committed in full knowledge of the act, or in ignorance? Was there a transformation from ignorance to knowledge? And finally: Was there any postcrime redemption?

SEVENTEEN

Ralph and Adam

The man said, "The woman whom thou gavest to be with me, she gave me fruit of the tree, and I ate."—Old Testament, Genesis 3:12

I'm mad as hell. The goddamn Giants took food off our table.—Ralph Branca

And speaking of scapegoating, another memorable exemplar of a perpetrator not yet mentioned was the first human on Earth, according to the Old Testament. As the above initial epigraph reflects, when asked by God, "Have you eaten of the tree of which I commanded you not to eat?" Adam scapegoated his innocent female partner and blamed his sin on her, refusing to take responsibility. (For the record, Eve then instantly became the world's second official scapegoat perpetrator, passing the inculpation hot potato, in turn, to the snake: "The serpent beguiled me, and I ate.")

Like Adam, Ralph Branca felt the natural and human need to have a scapegoat for his "crime," so he first blamed it not on Eve, but on the dimensions of the Polo Grounds, on the "cheap home run," and then on the Giants for cheating. But he actually went further than that at one point, placing the blame on God. When, during an interview at a country club in Westchester County, journalist Joshua Prager tells Branca about the members of the latter's family who died in the concentration camps and discusses the fact that Ralph was Jewish because, according to Jewish law, his mother—Kati, née Berger—was (the former pitcher only learned about this much later in life), Branca replies, "Maybe that's why God's mad at me—that I didn't practice my mother's religion. *He made me* throw that home run pitch..." (my italics). The revelatory statement did not appear to be made tongue in cheek.

Adam's crime was his disobedience to God and, taking his cue from Eve, his eating from the Tree of the Knowledge of Good and Evil.

Part Four—Crimes and Punishments

But it was betraying God's trust in him that principally led to his banishment from Eden. Branca, too, betrayed trust, to his way of thinking: his trust of himself, of his teammates, and of those rabid Brooklyn fans. And maybe of God, too.

In addition to the scapegoat and crime commonalities, a third intriguing parallel between Adam and Ralph relates to their knowledge of good and evil. Adam had no awareness of the two entities prior to chomping on the apple but became well acquainted with them (via his and Eve's sudden consciousness of their nakedness) soon thereafter; Ralph, on the other hand, was well aware that he had committed a baseball "sin" at the exact moment of his action and in fact used the precise and telling terms—albeit hyperbolic and pilfered from the Bard—*good* and *evil* to describe his transgression in his afterword to Bobby Thomson's memoir, even equating his plight (referring to himself in the third person, no less) to that of the tragic Roman emperor:

> I'm far from a Shakespeare buff, but I remembered reading a quotation from Julius Caesar. "The evil that men do lives after them, the good is oft interred with their bones." So be it with Caesar; so be it with Branca.

There are also the punishments of Adam and Ralph to consider, but first, a few words about "punishments fitting crimes."

The concept—referred to as lex talionis, or the law of retribution—was probably first expressed in around 1750 BC, in the Code of Hammurabi in Babylonian times. In the Old Testament, it appears in Exodus 21: 23–25: "If any harm follows, then you shall give life for life, eye for eye, tooth for tooth, hand for hand, foot for foot, burn for burn, wound for wound, stripe for stripe." And similar language is repeated in Leviticus 24: 19–21. Other incarnations of the lex talionis, among many others, pop up in the writings of Cicero (*Noxiae poena par esto*, "Let the punishment fit the crime," in his *De Legibus*), the Eighth Amendment of the U.S. Constitution ("Excessive bail shall not be required, nor excessive fines imposed, nor cruel and unusual punishments inflicted"), and Gilbert and Sullivan in *The Mikado* ("My object all sublime/I shall achieve in time—/To let the punishment fit the crime...").

Adam's penalty was meted out from the outside (God); in Genesis 3:17–19, he is punished thus: "...cursed is the ground because of you ... thorns and thistles it shall bring/forth to you ... you shall eat bread/till you return to the ground,/for out of it you were taken;/you are dust,/and to dust you shall return." Adam's God was meting out a pretty harsh but

SEVENTEEN. Ralph and Adam

proportionate punishment, and a fair one, a divine justice, for disobedience and loss of trust. Because of their monumental (but so "human") transgression, Adam and Eve clearly didn't deserve to remain in Eden or merit their blissful existence or live forever. Branca's punishment, conversely, came principally from the inside, from his own anger and sensitivity toward his being made the goat of The Game, and obviously wasn't as severe as Adam's. He punished himself internally, sporadically but for over sixty years, because of one unfortunate pitch, a far cry from Adam's blatant misdeed. But still, like Adam, his purely idyllic existence was denied (if he had only gotten Bobby out, and out of the inning!), but by his own making.

Regarding the issue of redemption, for Adam, despite the fact that his punishment involved fighting weeds and thistles while toiling with the earth (and Eve had to endure the pain of childbirth, to boot), the good news is that they both got to experience joy out of, and in contrast to, their misery, which gave it meaning and context, for them and for the human race to follow. And postexpulsion, Adam got to live to the ripe old age of 930.

Which constitutes yet another parallel the First Man shared with Everyman Ralph Branca: despite the fact that the latter's punishment involved inner disquietude and regret and "never getting paroled" for so long, the good news is that he got to experience lots of "redemptive" joy in his life and to live to the ripe old age of 90 (he passed away in 2016). And not only that, but according to some accounts, Biblical ages, if divided by ten, may be converted to modern-day ages, so if Adam lived to 930 and Branca to nearly 91, well, you do the math.

But all this is only half of my Adam/Branca story...

> *"Curiouser and curiouser!" cried Alice...*
> —Lewis Carroll, *Alice's Adventures in Wonderland*

Many decades ago, I found myself in the charming Brancacci Chapel in Florence, staring at the unbearably evocative ca. 1425 Masaccio fresco titled *Cacciata dei progenitori dall'Eden* (*Expulsion from the Garden of Eden*). It had been nearly thirty years since, in my freshman Art 101 course at Williams College, I first laid eyes on it. Even back then, in the form of a humble slide on a projection screen, its transformative power capturing the human spirit's vulnerability, in a spectacular moment of shame and angst, had a profound effect on me. But seeing it up close and personal was a whole different ball game. So there I am in the Brancacci

Part Four—Crimes and Punishments

Adam and Eve in Masaccio's fresco *Cacciata dei progenitori dall'Eden*, Brancacci Chapel, Florence.

Chapel, mesmerized by the image of Adam and Eve after they were booted—apparently unceremoniously—out of the Garden.

Eve is, to be sure, a startling figure, with her hollow, sunken, shamed eyes, her mournful mouth agape, her limp hands guiltily covering her erogenous zones; but it is Adam that I am, for some reason, focusing on. The hunched shoulders! The hands covering the face! The shame of it all! And then, out of the blue and without warning—as often happens in life, or at least in my brain—I am brutally attacked by an ineffably astounding and unannounced epiphany: perhaps because I am such an incurable baseball nut and many analogies I tend to summon up have their sources in this realm, my mind suddenly and instinctively jumps from Adam to—cross my heart and hope to die—the award-winning 1951 Barney Stein black-and-white photo of the sports goat of all time, Ralph Branca.

In my mind and in the photo, Branca—moments after giving up baseball's most famous gopher ball in

SEVENTEEN. Ralph and Adam

the most momentous and culturally important sporting event in history at the very end of the third and deciding pennant playoff game on October 3, 1951, to the immortal "Flying Scot," New York Giants third baseman Bobby Thomson—is sitting on the steps of the Brooklyn Dodgers clubhouse (whereas, in the fresco, Adam is standing), but the resemblance between this ridiculously unlikely pair is still extraordinary and unmistakable. The same arched back and slumped, dejected shoulders! The same hope-dashed face hidden sorrowfully in shadow! The same perfectly parallel arms and perfectly symmetrical hands clasped and frozen together! The same palpable and crushing feeling of shame! (And, by the way and not unremarkably, both Masaccio and Branca happened to be of Italian heritage.)

And the analogy continues to dimensionalize itself in my brain. And I suddenly hear Ernie Harwell's voice on my little 12-inch Dumont TV on 10/3/51, proclaiming, "It's ... *gone!*" and then I realize, suddenly, the parallel fates of Adam and Ralph: Adam (with Eve) is *gone*, tossed out of Eden, and his innocence is *gone*, and *gone* is his idyllic existence in paradise; and Harwell's "It's ... gone!" refers, literally, to Bobby's drive over the left-field fence, but figuratively, we can also imagine that it also implies that Branca is *gone*, tossed out of *his* Eden, and his innocence is *gone*, and *gone* is his idyllic existence in paradise.

And I am thinking, upon further rumination regarding this whole fantastic, improbable coincidence, about how both Adam and Ralph betrayed their trust and that they

A depressed Ralph Branca in the Dodgers' clubhouse, shortly after The Pitch dramatically ended the 10/3/51 pennant playoff game.

Part Four—Crimes and Punishments

are both punished for their "sins," Adam with expulsion and Ralph from his own lips ("I've never been paroled") with internal imprisonment, the result of throwing "that goddamn pitch." (Is it really a coincidence that he takes The Lord's name in vain?) Betrayal, loss, and punishment: funny how losing in baseball can sometimes earn Biblical status.

But, hard to believe, the best is yet to come. It is also at this very moment that I realize something beyond coincidence, an otherworldly confluence of two utterly unassociated phenomena that would have rendered even the great Rod Serling himself dumbstruck: it suddenly occurs to me that the Masaccio fresco—the absolute epitome of *the shame of loss*—is, permanently and for all time, housed in the chapel whose name is.... *BRANCAcci!*

Go figure.

EIGHTEEN

Ralph and Job

God damn the day I was born...
—Old Testament, Job 3:3

...that goddamn pitch...—Ralph Branca

Like the Biblical Adam, the Biblical Job shares a surprising number of fascinating commonalities with the non–Biblical Ralph Branca that reveal, when compared, the humanity, vulnerability, and basic goodness and piety of the Dodgers pitcher.

To—quite literally—make a very long story very short, in his eponymous and unspeakably poetic Old Testament book, Job is a righteous and pious (and also wealthy) man whose righteousness and piety (and wealth) are sorely tested by God. In heaven, then-angel Satan challenges God by stating that Job wouldn't be so pious if God took everything away from him, which God then allows Satan to do—health, wealth, property, animals, children, the whole shebang: everything but Job's actual life. After much complaining about the injustice of it all (Job did absolutely *nothing* wrong to deserve this horrific punishment) and suffering unspeakable mental and physical misery, Job never curses God directly or loses faith but ultimately accepts God's punishment and passes the "faith test," for which, in the end, he is rewarded mightily.

The "punishment fits the crime" theme is considered nowhere in more elegant detail than in the Book of Job, considered one of the "Books of Wisdom" along with Proverbs, Psalms, and Ecclesiastes. The reason why Job's punishment by God doesn't fit the crime whatsoever is that Job committed no crime. On the contrary, God was testing his faith (as He does often in the Old Testament, like when He tested Abraham's by asking him to sacrifice his son, Isaac) in a "bet" with Satan that Job would remain pious and faithful despite all the sorrow and devastation the then-angel and later-devil could produce. So, Job's is a horrific punishment for no crime at all.

Part Four—Crimes and Punishments

Similarly, Ralph Branca committed no crime except for (in his mind and that of many of his fans) tossing one unfortunate fastball that ended up where he didn't want it to. The subsequent discrepancy between crime (none) and punishment (six decades of regret and mental torment) is considerable, although not nearly as dramatic as that of the Biblical character.

Then there is the issue of undeserved suffering for these two pious men. For Job, who is innocent of any wrongdoing, it seems impossible for him to know why there is suffering coming his way, especially if it is unmerited and doled out by the hand of God:

> I am guiltless, but his mouth condemns me;
> blameless, but his words convict me.

And, further:

> Why have you made me your target
> and burdened me with myself?

This suggests the familiar "only the good die young" topos (expressed through the ages, from Greek mythology to Billy Joel): why are good people punished? Job's additional take, presenting the obverse side of the issue:

> Why do the wicked prosper
> and live to a ripe old age?

For Ralph, a good and pious man like Job, it always seems to revert to the "Why me?" conundrum that he first articulated to Father Rowley in the Polo Grounds parking lot right after the game. As he states, rhetorically but also perplexedly, in the afterword of Bobby's memoir, "So what was it? Fate? Destiny? Who knows?" The suffering of Ralph, from his perspective, seems always due to some outside force, and, like Job, the ultimate question often comes down to "Why, of all people, has God chosen me to punish?"

> *But why me, Father?*

A corollary to this issue of undeserved punishment is that of injustice: Job complains constantly about his unmerited punishment, blaming God for treating him unjustly (while never cursing God, his tormentor):

> He hands the earth to the wicked
> and blindfolds its judges' eyes....

EIGHTEEN. Ralph and Job

And:

> No—because God has tricked me,
> and lured me into his trap.
> I call, but there is no answer;
> I cry out, and where is justice?

Branca, too, speaks often of the unfairness of it all, in his case, the public and historical final judgment of him and his nemesis, Bobby. As he expresses it toward the end of his memoir:

As decades went by, the labels [goat, hero] became permanent; they were seared in the public imagination. The perception was unalterable:

> Bobby won it; I lost it.

Not unimportantly, both Job and Ralph, respectively, use the metaphor of the prison to characterize the injustice of their unmerited punishments:

> Man's life is a prison;
> he is sentenced to pain and grief.

> You know, if you kill somebody, they sentence you to life. You serve twenty years and you get paroled. I've never been paroled.

The reaction to punishment with anger is yet another commonality shared by the two "wronged" men. After sitting with his three friends (Eliphaz, Bildad, and Zophar) in silence and pain for seven days and seven nights, Job finally speaks, angrily and in no uncertain terms, regarding his suffering:

> I sit and gnaw on my grief;
> my groans pour out like water.
> My worst fears have happened;
> My nightmares have come to life.

The most significant difference between Job's and Branca's anger management is that whereas Job voiced—unabashedly, unrestrainedly, stentoriously—his rage and outrage from the beginning of his punishment until the end, when he embraced acceptance, Ralph struggled with his anger and resentment and punishment for nearly five decades (from 1954, when he learned about the cheating scandal from his Tigers teammate Ted Gray, until his tongue was "loosened" by Prager's 2001 *WSJ* piece), attempting to restrain and conceal his inner fury with silence, as he states in the introduction to his memoir:

Part Four—Crimes and Punishments

> I saw silence as my shield of dignity. I wanted to shout "Fraud!" but my nature wouldn't allow it.

And later, after he first learned about the cheating scandal, he tells his brother John:

> "Of course I'm mad. I'm mad as hell. The goddamn Giants took food off our table.... What they did was scandalous, but I don't want to be the one who breaks the scandal. That's not me..."

And again, in the next paragraph:

> There never should have been a playoff. We fought and won the pennant, only to get robbed.

Also intriguing are the parallel allusions to the loss of sleep as the two express their anger. First Job:

> If I say, "Sleep will comfort me,
> I will lie down to ease my pain,"
> Then you terrify me with visions,
> Your nightmares choke me with horror,
> And I wake up gasping for breath,
> Longing to be dead at last.

And then Branca's description after hearing the Wollensak telescope news from Ted Gray:

> I couldn't sleep that night. I couldn't sleep the next night. I kept tossing and turning.

Finally, what about the issue of redemption and whether or not it comes at the end of their stories? At the conclusion of his Biblical Book, Job totally accepts God in all His wisdom, even though he still clings to his persistent claims of innocence. And for this, Job was rewarded handsomely (after God had proven his point and Job had passed his test of faith, of course). So after Job did nothing to deserve his punishment and then complained mightily and then finally accepted God's punishment, after all that, he was rewarded with 14,000 sheep, 6,000 camels, 1,000 yoke of oxen, 1,000 donkeys, 7 sons, and 3 daughters (the most beautiful in all the world), and he lived to see his grandchildren and great-grandchildren and died at a very great age, probably over the age of 200.

And Ralph? For his "noncrime," he received no reward from his God—although he was a deeply religious man—in the form of an answer

EIGHTEEN. Ralph and Job

Engraving in William Blake's *Illustrations of the Book of Job*.

to his "Why me?" query. No parole, either, as he put it. Where Job exhibited acceptance, Branca displayed resignation. And where Job found faith, Ralph, a man of deep faith, was never able to be fully at peace with his or to receive an answer to the question he asked God to resolve and that continued to haunt him until the end.

Part Four—Crimes and Punishments

Tellingly (especially in the context of this chapter), in his August 15, 2011, *New York Times* piece, during that interview of Branca at a Westchester County country club, Joshua Prager described Branca's guilty reaction to learning later in life that he was Jewish in the following way (my italics): "He was smiling but sincere, *a Job* wondering about the root of his suffering."

NINETEEN

Ralph and Oedipus

All human happiness or misery takes the form of action ... it is in our actions—what we do—that we are happy or the reverse.—Aristotle, *Poetics*

It pains me to be remembered for one unfortunate pitch...
—Ralph Branca

Surely it would seem like unadulterated hyperbole to compare Ralph Branca to Oedipus and to conclude that they were both tragic heroes. And yet.

Ralph Branca was not strictly a tragic hero in various ways and on the surface, but if we examine the situation of the protagonist of Sophocles' *Oedipus Rex*, the commonalities shared by the King of Thebes and the Goat of Coogan's Bluff will prove striking, and it will be instructive to compare who they were and what—because of and in spite of themselves—befell them.

To explore this unlikely analogy, we need to begin—and end—with Aristotle's treatise on Greek dramatic theory, *Poetics*. The part of this opus that concerns us here in terms of the Oedipus/Branca commonalities is the description of the traits of the tragic hero (tellingly, Aristotle chooses Oedipus as his ideal protagonist) and how his actions affect both him and the audience watching him.

Among the Aristotelian characteristics of the tragic hero shared by Oedipus and Branca, the following five are the most salient:

Hamartia: a tragic flaw in a man of eminence and noble nature. As far as a similarity between Oedipus and Ralph is concerned, they were both upstanding citizens and men of excellent character. Regarding their "nobility," the parents of Oedipus, Laius and Jocasta, were royalty (king and queen); and Ralph's, although not royal, came from Italian (father John) and Jewish (mother Kati) roots, which represent, like Oedipus' Greek roots, ancient and noble cultures.

Part Four—Crimes and Punishments

The "tragic flaw" to which Aristotle refers has to do with some weakness of character, moral blindness, or *error in judgment or action* (my italics; the term *hamartia* literally means "missing the mark"). Now, for most people, there is often one traumatic event in their lives (the death of a friend or relative, a health issue, a natural disaster, etc.) that leaves a scar in their psyches and affects how they view the world and gives them a special sense of perspective. But for tragic heroes in general and Oedipus and Ralph in particular, their *hamartia* was about an error, an act, that they committed, not a trauma that happened to them outside of themselves. For Oedipus, his flaw was his disobedience, his disregard of the oracular prediction, and, oh, his murdering his father and marrying his mother and his subsequent hubris, or excessive arrogance, in thinking he could "outrun his fate"; Ralph's error was throwing the fatal fastball and then exhibiting hubris in espousing the cheating scandal as an escape hatch for his act. *All human happiness or misery takes the form of action ... it is in our actions—what we do—that we are happy or the reverse.*

To be more specific, according to Aristotle, *hamartia* is not found in the characters of the tragic heroes, in their depravity or vice (in which case the audience would lose respect for them), but in some "error" or "mistake." Although according to Aristotle, *hamartia* has no "evil intent" attached to it, Oedipus did not bear responsibility for his error (he refused to believe the prophecy that he killed his father and married his mother); similarly, Ralph responded with relief and gratitude to the cheating scandal and openly accepted the Giants as his scapegoat.

Another manifestation—a by-product, actually—of *hamartia* is anger. For Oedipus, it was anger at his father, Laius (whose parental identity had not yet been revealed), during an earlier encounter, whom he kills; and at Tiresias, the blind prophet, whom he insults regarding his blindness (how ironic!). For Branca, it was his "long-suppressed rage," as he put it, directed toward the Giants, Leo Durocher, and the treatment he received, mostly from disgruntled Dodgers fans.

Peripeteia: a reversal of fortune, good to bad. The parallel development in the two protagonists: the downfall of a once-mighty king (Oedipus) and the downfall of a once-mighty pitcher (Ralph).

A second feature of *Peripeteia* is a change of fortune that "must ... come about, not through depravity, but through a serious defect in judgment..."; both Oedipus and Ralph were good, honorable men, and both made terrible choices (albeit unwittingly and not deliberately): the

NINETEEN. Ralph and Oedipus

father/mother thing and the choice of throwing the fastball. And consequently, both suffered, according to Aristotle's description of *peripeteia*, from an "undeserved misfortune" that outweighed the action itself. Both Oedipus and Ralph had everything to look forward to until disaster struck.

Anagnorisis: a discovery (literally, "knowing again"), a revelation, a change from ignorance to knowledge. For Oedipus, obviously, this element relates to the horrific discovery of the secret—revealed to him by the blind prophet Tiresias (the irony of his blindness, which portends Oedipus' blinding himself, is not lost to the audience)—that he has, unknowingly, murdered his father, Laius, and married his mother, Jocasta.

In Branca's case, his discovery, through a revelation, of the Giants cheating scandal led to his hubris, or the Aristotelian arrogance he adopted by blaming it all on Bobby Thomson's purported foreknowledge (another Oedipal element: the King of Thebes, too, like Bobby, had no foreknowledge of his dual dastardly deeds), by not believing Bobby's insistence that he never did see the fastball sign.

Pathos: suffering, the result of a destructive or painful act. Oedipus was destined to be shunned for, and punished by, his horrific actions, and of course he suffered unimaginably for them. Ralph, for his part, also suffered internally, quite a bit and for a long time, not only his own version of exile and obloquy (reviled and ridiculed by fans and the press), but also his inner feelings of regret and self-blame.

Add to this the fact that for both protagonists, the suffering never ends: before he dies, Oedipus lives on after his self-blinding, is exiled from Thebes to Colonus a blind and broken man, and places curses on his sons, Polyneices and Eteocles (they end up killing each other in battle). His only solace is the love and fidelity of his daughter, Antigone. Likewise, Ralph's *pathos* will surface and resurface and continue to the end. He is solaced through it all by his loving wife, Ann, and his family and friends. This quote from *Oedipus Rex* could apply to the suffering of both men: "Count no man happy till he dies, free of pain at last." And this one from *A Moment in Time* drives home the point of continual suffering:

> After my retirement from pro ball, I was sure again that The Pitch would eventually be forgotten. I was wrong again.

Catharsis: the relieving effect that a tragic act has on the audience, eliciting the emotions of pity (*eleos:* what they feel at a misfortune that is

Part Four—Crimes and Punishments

out of proportion to the faults of a man) and fear (*phobos*: what they feel when misfortune comes upon one like themselves). According to Aristotle, the audience develops an emotional attachment to and sympathy for the hero, pities what happens to him, and fears him because it could befall anyone. Such is the audience's reaction to the tragic acts of Oedipus; such is the reaction of baseball fans since 10/3/51 who, although many revile him for his act, can still empathize with Branca's misfortune. Both reactions are caused by the punishments of the two protagonists that are greater than they deserve. And finally, Oedipus arouses pity at the end when he blinds himself (literally) instead of killing himself, and Ralph arouses pity when he blinds himself (figuratively) to taking full responsibility for his "misdeed," preferring to blame it on the Giants cheating scandal.

Simply put, then, Ralph Branca actually fits quite neatly into every one of these Aristotelian tragic-hero criteria originally ascribed to characters like Oedipus. But beyond the characteristics of the tragic hero shared by Oedipus and Branca, two additional factors deserve special mention.

Fate: This is the subject in Aristotle's discussion of Sophocles' *Oedipus at Colonus* (the last of the three "Theban plays" that Sophocles wrote, the other two being *Oedipus Rex* and *Antigone*), where Oedipus declares that even though fate (*dike*), which literally means "necessity" in ancient Greek, is something we must suffer as beyond our choice in its power of necessity and is not a person's creation, we must also find a way to work with it. The key line in the play is when Oedipus declares, "Let us not fight necessity," and Antigone adds, "For you will never see in all the world a man whom God has let escape his destiny." Does this ring a baseball bell? Ralph's quote ("So what was it? Fate? Destiny? Who knows?"), in this context, seems so Aristotelian. Although it was said innocently, it does have "Greek tragedy" overtones.

Nomenclature: This one Aristotle doesn't mention, but I will throw it in as a bonus element because it offers us some fascinating coincidences. Oedipus' name has as its etymological roots the Greek words *oida* ("swollen") and *pous* ("foot") because when the future king was a baby, his father, Laius, to avoid the oracular prophecy that his own son would kill him, pierced Oedipus' ankles and tethered them (leaving lasting scars), after which the baby was left by a servant on a mountain to die. By pure analogical chance, the word *branca* means "claw hand" or "paw" in Italian, and, to boot, it can mean "foot" in Latin.

NINETEEN. Ralph and Oedipus

Not only that, but *branca* also means "white" (the "innocence" of both Oedipus and Ralph) in Portuguese and "protect" in Croatian (Oedipus tried to protect his nonbiological parents, Polybus and Merope, by fleeing Corinth; Ralph Branca was protecting his Dodgers' lead in the bottom of the ninth).

Further, Ralph's nickname was "The Hawk," meant to describe his strong, prominent proboscis. But it also happens to be, coincidentally, the bird that symbolizes certain Oedipal qualities: courage in Native American culture, protection in Cheyenne tribal lore, and prophecy (the many prophecies in *Oedipus Rex*; the ostensible forecasting of the signs to Thomson by Yvars) in Norse and Greek mythology.

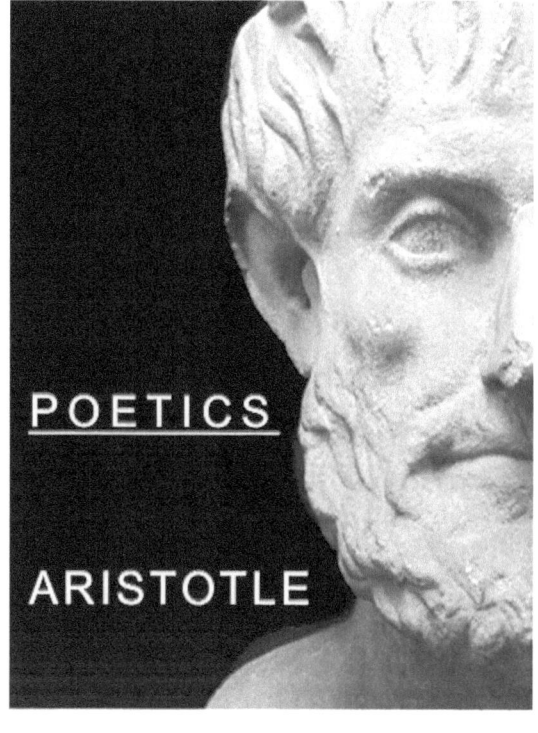

One of many book covers of Aristotle's *Poetics*, in which he defines the tragic hero.

Concerning the "crime and punishment" comparison between Oedipus and Ralph, there is a case to be made for similarity and comparability. Oedipus committed two of the most unimaginable crimes without any knowledge of the true identity of his victims. He fulfilled the prophecy unbeknownst to him and was thus "innocent" of any horrendous wrongdoing or premeditation. This is the great irony of the entire tragedy. So on the one hand, the punishment fit the crime (on the face of the crime itself); but on the other, more important hand, and according to the Aristotelian guidelines, it was unspeakably unjust and unmerited and way out of proportion to the crime itself (and the reason the audience had to feel pity and thus *catharsis*).

Part Four—Crimes and Punishments

By the same token, Ralph's "crime" was an innocent one not meant to hurt himself or anyone else; and although The Pitch did require that he take responsibility for his act, the consequences (opprobrium, obloquy, self-torture, obsession) were unspeakably unjust and unmerited and way out of proportion to the crime itself.

TWENTY

Ralph and Hester

> And, after many, many years, a new grave was delved ... and on this simple slab of slate.... "ON A FIELD, SABLE, THE LETTER A, GULES."—Nathaniel Hawthorne, *The Scarlet Letter*
>
> *I'm going to hear about Bobby's homer until the day they put me in the grave.*—Ralph Branca

At first blush, the names *Ralph Branca* and *Hester Prynne* appearing together in the same sentence—as they do in this one—might seem oddly far-fetched. Hester, the protagonist in Nathaniel Hawthorne's novel *The Scarlet Letter*, is a woman, she commits a crime, her crime is adultery, her oppressors are her Puritan neighbors, she is shunned and lives her life in solitude, and her punishment is concrete and symbolized by a red-colored piece of material embroidered on her clothing above her chest. Branca, on the contrary, is a man, he commits no "real" crime, his oppressors are himself and the press and his fans, he is shunned but lives his life surrounded by loving family and friends, and his punishment is abstract and symbolized by an announcer's play-by-play radio recording.

For our purposes, though, luckily there is always a second blush.

The Scarlet Letter recounts the (mostly) sad tale of Hester Prynne, a young woman who conceives a daughter, Pearl, with a man to whom she is not married and then, in the face of abusive shunning by her Puritan Massachusetts community and being forced by them—for life—to wear a scarlet *A* (the red stain of sin, standing for "Adultery") on the bosom of her dress for all to see, struggles to create a new existence based on self-reliance and dignity.

The two main supporting characters in this morality story are Arthur Dimmesdale, the town minister and father to Pearl, who is racked with internal shame and guilt by the secret "sin" he committed

Part Four—Crimes and Punishments

with Hester (at the end of the novel, he reveals his sin during a sermon, then dies in Hester's arms); and Roger Chillingsworth, Hester's husband, presumed dead, who seeks revenge—again, the lex talionis—on Dimmesdale, becomes his physician, and conducts a campaign of psychological torture against the minister before dying, weak and drained, soon after Dimmesdale's death.

While it is true that ostensibly, committing adultery and throwing a fastball seem to have precious little in common in terms of their criminality, one similarity Hester and Ralph share in this regard—and one that is not shared by any of the "criminals" discussed in the preceding pages, i.e., Adam, Job, and Oedipus—is the element of schadenfreude that accompanies their punishments.

Etymologically, the word *schadenfreude* is a combination of the German words *Schaden* (harm) and *Freude* (joy, used most notably by Beethoven in the fourth movement of his Ninth Symphony, in the "Ode to Joy," based in part on the ode by Friedrich Schiller titled *"An die Freude"*). So in essence, schadenfreude means finding joy in someone else's misfortune, which is one of the most human of feelings, or wishing for the failure of one's opponents (as in those old Dodgers fans wishing for the failure of the Giants, and vice versa).

For Hester Prynne, the metaphorical reminder of her sin—the embroidered scarlet *A*—is accompanied by the joy that members of her Puritan community take in her suffering, clearly apparent in their various comments in the marketplace scene, Chapter 2:

"Ah, but," interposed a young wife, holding a child by the hand, "let her cover the mark as she will, the pang of it will be always in her heart."

And (shouted by "another female, the ugliest as well as the most pitiless of these self-constituted judges"):

"This woman has brought shame upon us all, and ought to die. Is there not law for it?"

And (muttered by "the most iron-visaged of the old dames"):

"It were well ... if we stripped Madam Hester's rich gown off her dainty shoulders; and as for the red letter, which she hath stitched so curiously, I'll bestow a rag of mine own rheumatic flannel, to make a fitter one!"

And (cried out by "the grim beadle"):

"A blessing on the righteous Colony of the Massachusetts, where inequity is dragged out into the sunshine! Come along, Madam Hester, and show your scarlet letter in the market-place!"

TWENTY. Ralph and Hester

For Ralph Branca, the metaphorical (but very real!) reminder of his "sin"—for him and, in the spirit of schadenfreude, for millions of Giants fans and even for some Dodgers fans—was the 78 rpm recording of the Thomson homer, a special release on the Chesterfield label, by the radio play-by-play announcer that day, Russ Hodges (as a kid, I actually owned this record and played it hundreds of times, to my adolescent, rabid– Giants-fan delight):

> The Giants win the pennant!
> The Giants win the pennant!
> The Giants win the pennant!
> The Giants win the pennant!

Hodges' sound bite of quadruple hysteria and jubilation—which served to thrill Giants fans across the country and to rub it in for Dodgers fans (but also, as an auditory act of schadenfreude, to justify Ralph as their scapegoat for the Dodgers' loss)—never ceased to echo in the ear of Ralph Branca for the rest of his life: Hodges' searing, ebullient words became for him not only a symbol of the fodder for schadenfreude, for the "rubbing it in" fans could feel toward him, but also that of Ralph's own anguish, his distress every time he heard it as a recording or in his head, as he expresses it in his memoir:

> Every time I turned on the radio it seemed like that was all I heard. I did well not to throw the damn radio through the window.

And again, in the afterword of Bobby Thomson's memoir:

> As the years passed, the home run kept coming up again and again. I remember in 1976, I went to old-timers' days in Texas and San Diego. It was the twenty-fifth anniversary of Bobby's home run that year and in both places they played Russ Hodges's famous call: *"The Giants win the pennant! The Giants win the pennant!"* They didn't tell me ahead of time because they probably figured I would veto it. I remember Pee Wee Reese coming over to me after they played it and saying, "Man, you must be awful sick of that stuff." And, in truth, I was.

In both *The Scarlet Letter* and that other tale of schadenfreude and woe, the 10/3/51 game, and its subsequent reverberations, the "scapegoat element" is palpably present. In the Hawthorne novel, the Puritan townsfolk need a scapegoat (hence, Hester's severe lifetime punishment), which allows them to harbor the pretense of their own moral purity while punishing her for a sin of which they are all capable. With Ralph, the Dodgers pitcher needed a scapegoat (the Giants cheating

Part Four—Crimes and Punishments

scandal) to "loosen his tongue," to exculpate himself from total responsibility, and to soothe the guilt for his "sin."

There also exists a similarity between the two protagonists in terms of the nature of their punishments: in both cases, ostracism—as part of the schadenfreude just discussed—played a significant role.

In Hester's case, her shunning by her Massachusetts neighbors constitutes the essence of the radical punishment for her sin of adultery. Puritan society in the seventeenth century was a tough crowd, way tougher and more punitive-leaning than twentieth-century Brooklyn Bums fans, as reflected in their lifetime punishment (ostracism, wearing her scarlet *A*) exacted on Hester for the crime of her adultery:

> It [the scarlet letter] had the effect of a spell, taking her out of the ordinary relations with humanity, and enclosing her in a sphere by herself.

For Ralph, the punishment was less severe, of course, and consisted of his own regret and anger as well as his ostracism by disgruntled and angry fans. He could actually have been wearing his own (internal) scarlet *A*, which for him would have stood for *Aspirin* (as in Aspirin tablet, or a fastball in baseball vernacular). In one of the various passages in Ralph's memoir that describe his abuse, ignominy, schadenfreude, and shunning, the following exchange transpires between Ralph and a few disgruntled fans (in 1955, at the end of his baseball career, while Ralph was pitching for the AAA—triple-A!—farm club of, ironically, his longtime nemesis NY Giants—the Minneapolis Millers—and giving up eight home runs in spring training):

> "Hey, Branca!" one [fan] screamed. "Where's your buddy Thomson?"
> "Is it true," yelled another, "that *you're banned* [my italics] from Brooklyn for life?"
> "You're a sad sack!"
> "You're a has-been!"
> "You're a bum!"
> Finally, I turned to those jerks and let 'em have it: "What ball team have you played on? The Bloomer Girls?"

The use of the word *nightmare* to describe the haunting quality of their punishments is yet another point of similarity between Hester and Ralph, first employed by Roger Chillingsworth and directed toward Hester:

> How is it, Hester? Doth thy sentence bind thee to wear the token in thy sleep? Art thou not afraid of nightmares and hideous dreams?

TWENTY. Ralph and Hester

And then by Branca, in the chapter aptly titled "The White Handkerchief" in his memoir:

At home at night, I still had nightmares about that goddamn pitch. I couldn't wait for spring training.

We have already considered the similarities between Adam and Ralph as far as their crime-and-punishment situations are concerned. But the same comparison may be made between Hester (and, for that matter, Dimmesdale) and Ralph, in the context of Adam: a basically good, "innocent" person makes the wrong choice, commits a "sin," is expelled and loses his/her freedom (for Adam, expulsion from Eden by God; for Hester and Ralph, ostracism/shunning by society), and suffers great pain and punishment.

But on the positive side....

There is, first, the quality of honor that both Hester and Ralph display in the form of keeping a secret that would be hurtful to others and would go against the internal moral code they both possessed and to which they both adhered.

When commanded to confess and name her lover/the father of her child (Arthur Dimmesdale), Hester, to protect Dimmesdale and to follow her moral compass, refuses ("I will not speak!"), to which Dimmesdale remarks, "Wondrous strength and generosity of a woman's heart! She will not speak!"

Ralph, for his part, kept silent about the Giants scandal for fifty years (until Prager's breaking the story in 2001):

I didn't want to be seen as a whiner, a sore loser, or a baby crying over spilt milk. Take it on the chin. Accept the blow. Move on with your life. Or, best of all, forget about it, which proved impossible.

His silence, like Hester's, was honorable; yet—aside from the fact that his tongue was eventually loosened—his motivations for the silence were less pure than Hester's (note the six revealing, qualifying words, *I didn't want to be seen,* indicating his awareness of the importance of being judged by others).

Besides honor, there is the issue of redemption to consider. Hester finds it after accepting her shame (making lemonade out of lemons), and through her desire to start anew. She also rejects this shame by not only starting a new life, but also by embellishing the scarlet *A* on her dress with golden thread, putting her personal "signature" on her sin. (Later,

Part Four—Crimes and Punishments

over time, some of her neighbors even interpret the *A* as standing for *Able*, acknowledging her strength and independence.)

Ralph saw the Giants scandal as his redemption ... but not really. Like Hester, he never repented his "sin," but whereas she accepted and overcame it, he tried to but retained his anger and frustration over it.

Finally, and importantly, there is the salvatory presence of love. Arthur Dimmesdale (who dies not in conflict, but in a previously unknown sense of peace after his confession) and Hester (who has maintained her love for him) actually end up sharing a tombstone: "Yet one tombstone served for both," attested in the novel's final paragraph; and not only that, but the scarlet letter on the shared tombstone no longer represents a stigma, but rather a sign of redemption and love: "On a field, sable, the letter A, gules." Arthur and Hester's headstone is black, and the letter *A* is inscribed in scarlet (*gules* is the word for "red" in

One version of Hester Prynne's scarlet *A*.

TWENTY. Ralph and Hester

Record jacket of Russ Hodges' (in)famous radio call.

heraldry, from the French and medieval Latin word for "throat"). In the end, for both Hester and Ralph, the shame and ignominy and shunning are tempered, solaced, and soothed by love: Hester's unconditional love for both Dimmesdale and her daughter, Pearl; and Ralph's love, for and from, his wife, his children, his large family, and his dear friends. So essentially and unexpectedly, both *The Scarlet Letter* and "The Miracle at Coogan's Bluff" end up as love stories.

Perhaps it was neither Hawthorne nor Branca who put it most simply and eloquently and innocently, but the great John Lennon, in five of the simplest and most powerful lyrics he ever penned.
All you need is love.

TWENTY-ONE

Ralph and Rodion

> *Perhaps I've been unfair to myself... perhaps after all I am a man and not a louse and I've been in too great a hurry to condemn myself. I'll make another fight for it.*—Rodion Raskolnikov, in Dostoevsky's *Crime and Punishment*

> *"I blew it, Father..." "You're being too hard on yourself, son..." "But why me, Father? I love this game so much. Why did it have to be me?"*—Ralph Branca and Father Pat Rowley

It is probably not a stretch to posit that the literary work that most clearly represents the metaphor for crime and punishment is, well, *Crime and Punishment*.

On my list of favorite "classic" international novelists, I include Cervantes, Melville, Dickens, Flaubert, Woolf, Proust, and Joyce. But my first love (I think when I was in eighth grade) and near or at the top of my list is Fyodor Dostoevsky's magnificent 1866 tale of psychological depth and human introspection.

In this iconic Russian novel, former law student Rodion Romanovich Raskolnikov, living in a garret in St. Petersburg and out of desperation and poverty and a sense that he is superior to the moral laws of society, cooks up a crime and carries it out, murdering (with an ax) an old woman, the loathsome pawnbroker Alyona Ivanovna, and then killing her mentally disabled half-sister, who witnessed the murderous act. This single (actually, double) act becomes the source of Raskolnikov's inner torment, guilt, paranoia, and self-degradation, which occupies the greater portion of the novel. His internal struggle is accompanied by many subplots, including Raskolnikov's love interest, the saintly Sonya Marmeladov, who is forced into prostitution to support her family; her urging Rodion to confess and unburden himself of his guilt; Rodion's

TWENTY-ONE. Ralph and Rodion

ultimate confession to Porfiry Petrovich, the cunning magistrate and lead investigator of the crime; his conviction and (light, considering the crime!) eight-year sentence to a prison in Siberia; Sonya's following him there out of love; and his incipient efforts, at the conclusion of the novel, to repent and to accept Sonya's love.

Any comparison between the crimes of Raskolnikov and Branca—a double murder vs. an errant fastball—would seem blatantly risible. In addition to the fact that Ralph's "crime" wasn't an actual crime, Rodion's—as opposed to those of the other protagonists discussed in previous chapters: Adam, Job, Oedipus, Hester—was grotesque and premeditated and thus even less seemingly analogous to Ralph's.

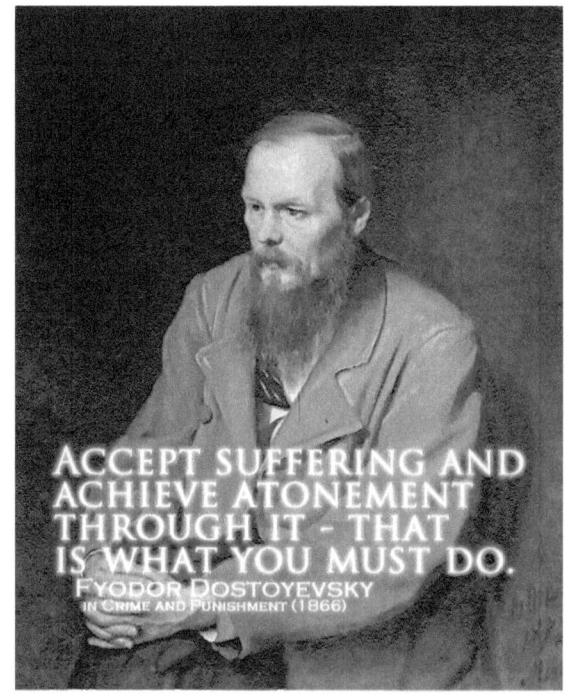

Good advice, from Rodion to Ralph.

What can be revealing here, however, is not the crimes of the protagonists of Dostoevsky's novel and the Miracle at Coogan's Bluff, but their consequences, the punishments exacted upon them.

The bottom line is that for both Rodion and Ralph, *punishments for a single act manifested themselves, similarly, in the form of internal struggles.* Which allows us to compare their respective situations from various perspectives:

• Ostensibly, both were punished by external forces (the Russian ex-student by the law and Porfiry's intense interrogation, the pitcher by the press and the fans), but the *real* punishments

Part Four—Crimes and Punishments

for both emanated from internal thoughts and feelings: for Rodion, severe personal torment, self-loathing, and wallowing in guilt; for Ralph, self-incrimination, internalized anger, and continuing regret.

- Rodion was constantly violating his conscience, not admitting the amorality of his crime, refusing to confess it, and paying the price emotionally. In a noteworthy analogy, by not taking full responsibility for his act—and using the Giants cheating scandal as a justification, an exoneration, an exculpation, a scapegoat—Ralph continued to be punished, in his mind, by the reappearing specter of The Pitch.
- The pressure exerted on Rodion Raskolnikov by his poverty and then by his keeping his act a secret led to paranoia, self-doubt, and alienation from society. Likewise, the pressure exerted on Ralph Branca to win, to perform in the Brooklyn hotbed of rabid fandom in the most important game of his life (and, in fact, of many of ours) led to alienation from society (the fans), guilt, regret, and anger.
- Regarding the common cause of their punishments, social pressures, once again, played a major role. For Rodion, the poverty in which he was mired pushed him to transcend moral laws, to be above them, to justify his extreme murderous act, to concoct the theory that "superior" men (like him) have the right to be above the law, to sidestep the societal rules of good and evil, and to get away at least for a while with murder, literally. For Ralph, as discussed, he paid the price for the fact that he cared so deeply about what his loyal, then turncoat, fans thought of him and how they judged his "sin."
- Ralph's punishment was more "unjust" than his counterpart's: whereas Rodion was not punished nearly as much as he should have been (he only received an eight-year sentence in Siberia for a capital punishment), Ralph was punished way more than he should have been (for having thrown that one "goddamn pitch").

A footnote to the preceding discussion: it is significant that in both cases, confessions represent pivotal moments. When Raskolnikov finally confesses his crime to Porfiry (after much hesitation and suspense), he experiences a release, an unburdening of his guilt; and when

TWENTY-ONE. Ralph and Rodion

Branca hears the confession of Tigers teammate Ted Gray about the cheating process utilized by the Giants, it results in a "loosening of the tongue," a discovery of a scapegoat, a sudden enlightenment.

And, perhaps recalling Adam's defiant munching on the apple, a sudden and unexpected knowledge of the difference between Good and Evil?

TWENTY-TWO

Ralph and Josef

Someone must have slandered Josef K., since, without having done any evil, he was arrested one morning.—Franz Kafka, *The Trial*

But why me, Father?—Ralph Branca, to Father Pat Rowley

Of all the literary protagonists whose plights might justifiably be compared to that of Ralph Branca, clearly the most bizarre and disturbing one is Josef K., the central character of Franz Kafka's *The Trial*. In fact, he is downright Kafkaesque.

The novel's basic plot is not that complicated: Josef K., a bank clerk, is charged with a crime that he never committed and then arrested (but not really); and at the end of the book, he is brutally executed by two unidentified men. That's about it. But the real meaning of the story is hidden, rather, in what does *not* happen and what is absent, which is *absurd*, in the deepest literary sense:

- Before all else, the facts are that many of the chapters in *The Trial* were either unfinished or deleted by Kafka and that before he died, he wanted the ms. to be destroyed (luckily, his literary executor and best friend, Max Brod, didn't honor his request).
- The novel was never completed, and the final version is still missing.
- Josef K. was arrested, but he was at the same time—oddly!—not arrested at all and instead was liberated, to resume his daily life.
- Josef's "crime" is never revealed, so he is never told why he is arrested and charged with it but is nonetheless adjudged guilty as charged.
- As the principal character, Josef isn't even given the courtesy of a last name, which is quite rare for the protagonists of novels, at least for those who are not the narrators.

TWENTY-TWO. Ralph and Josef

- Further, the agency that arrests him and the clerks and judges and agents and other members of the Court are never identified and remain anonymous throughout.
- Although the novel's title is *The Trial*, a trial never takes place, the Court's proceedings remain secret, and the legal "process" is mysterious and dilatory and constantly interrupted and replete with endless bureaucracy and red tape, all described in brutally objective detail in impossibly lengthy and excruciatingly detailed paragraphs.
- The German title, *Der Prozess*, is ambiguous: it could mean either "the trial" or "the process" (of the judicial system, but also of life itself, which is a constant trial and challenge for humans).
- While the trial is never taking place, the plot is filled with a series of interruptive actions such as sexual encounters, floggings, violence, and similar "delays," adding to the absurdity—and dark humor—of it all.

One of the commonalities shared by Josef K. and Ralph B. is the nonexistence of a real crime and yet the absolute absurdity of their subsequent punishments. Josef F.'s life is rendered absurd by the mental anguish caused by his (nonexistent) arrest and his (nonexistent) "trial." (Kafka believed in this absurdity of life, stating at one point that the human race was the product of one of "God's bad days.")

Similarly, Ralph B.'s punishment—by both himself and the fans—was absurdly out of proportion with the "crime" of throwing that fastball, a proverbial mountain made out of a molehill—or, in Ralph B.'s case, a literal mound. Ralph B. is obviously not, unlike Josef K., blamed for an act he didn't commit, but his punishment is, like Josef's, clearly out of proportion with his misdeed.

In the scheme of things juridical, there are, at the top, horrendous murders with justifiably harsh and deserved punishments (cf. Oedipus) and some less harsh but well deserved (e.g., Rodion). Next, there are laughably minor crimes with absurdly harsh punishments (in literature, the case that leaps to mind is that of Jean Valjean, the hero of Victor Hugo's *Les Misérables*, who stole a loaf of bread to feed his starving sister's kids and was sentenced to nineteen years in prison for that puny and morally justifiable indiscretion, before his ultimate redemption later in the novel). And then, there are those victims who are punished severely for committing no crime at all (viz., Josef K. and Ralph B.).

Part Four—Crimes and Punishments

In the case of Josef K., his punishment for committing no crime (inner torment, self-doubt, etc.) led to his self-destruction and then to his arbitrary and meaningless execution at the end: for no apparent reason, he is executed with a butcher's knife—stabbed in the heart—and strangled by two unidentified men, dying, as he says in the final paragraph, "like a dog!" (*Wie ein Hund!*"). These final words should recall the Linda Loman quote about husband Willy in *Death of a Salesman*: "He's not to be allowed to fall in his grave like an old dog. Attention, attention must finally be paid to such a person."

In the case of Ralph B., except for the execution scene and the self-destruction, the parallels with Josef K. are evident: Why me? What was my crime? The inner torment, the self-doubt, the internalizing of guilt. The punishment not fitting the crime. And for both Josef K. and Ralph B., there was no redemption in terms of the crime itself (although Ralph led a lot longer and happier life than Josef).

Of the other literary protagonists already considered, the closest comparable case is that of Job. Like Josef K. and Ralph B., Job was a victim of injustice, innocent of any conscious wrongdoing (as opposed to Adam, Oedipus, Hester, and Rodion). There was no crime, and thus no rationale for his punishment.

There is, further, a nightmarish quality hovering over, and

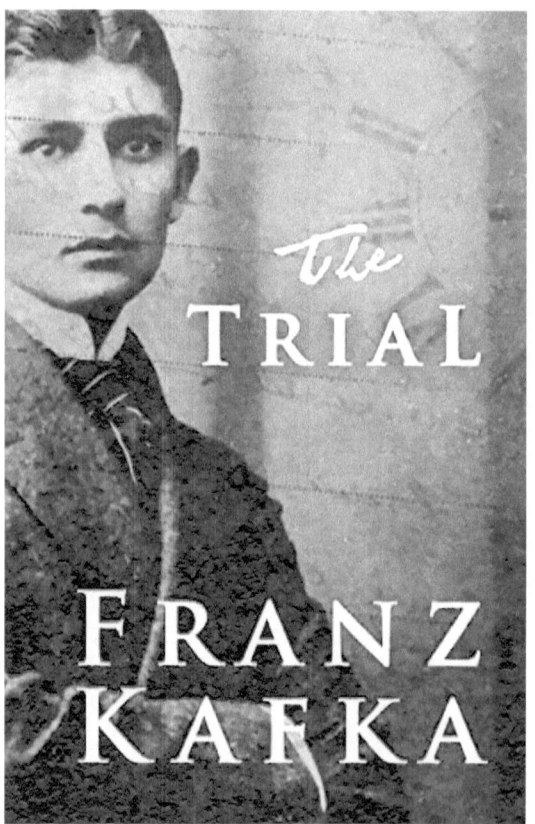

Book cover of Franz Kafka's *The Trial*.

TWENTY-TWO. Ralph and Josef

haunting, the existence of Josef K. (We also see this in another of Kafka's writings, the 1915 novella, *Die Werwandlung* or *The Metamorphosis*, in which traveling salesman—like Willy Loman!—Gregor Samsa wakes up one morning to find himself transformed into an enormous cockroach.) After his "arrest," Josef K.'s life, filled with mounting feelings of guilt, has the quality of a living nightmare.

To a lesser extent, certainly, but still comparable, is Ralph B.'s desultory obsession with his fateful act and his sleepless nights, including those that followed his learning of the Giants scandal:

> I couldn't sleep that night. I couldn't sleep the next night. I kept tossing and turning.

Or, as the Lord Chancellor expresses it in the frenetic and brilliant "Nightmare Song" in Gilbert and Sullivan's operetta *Iolanthe*:

> When you're lying awake with a dismal headache, and repose is taboo'd by anxiety...

Finally, there exists one significant common element in the crimes and punishments of all the protagonists—Adam, Job, Oedipus, Hester, Rodion, Josef K., Ralph B.—examined thus far: all have predetermined outcomes. In the "case" of Josef K., he is, absurdly, guilty as charged from the very beginning, although he never gives up his belief that he is innocent.

The same can be said, absurdly, about Ralph B.

TWENTY-THREE

Ralph and Sisyphus

Il faut imaginer Sisyphe heureux.—Albert Camus

The darkness of that day—October 3, 1951—has been overwhelmed by a life filled with light.—Ralph Branca

There is little question that life can sometimes appear absurd. For the French twentieth-century existentialist writers and philosophers, and for Albert Camus in particular, we can rephrase this tentative, heavily qualified proposition as the definitive and exclamatory cri de coeur "There is *no* question that life *is* absurd!" (Camus was, understandably, influenced by the absurdist views and writings of Franz Kafka, which were, in turn, influenced by Dostoevsky.)

Of the many literary examples that illustrate this passionate dictum—and how life's absurdity can actually be overcome and end in triumph—one of the most moving and powerful ones is Sisyphus, the magnificent antihero in Camus' 1942 philosophical essay *Le Mythe de Sisyphe* (*The Myth of Sisyphus*).

In Greek mythology, Sisyphus, king of Ephyra, had angered Zeus by cheating death (among other way more serious misbehaviors) and was punished for his misdeeds by being condemned for eternity to carrying a boulder up a hill only to see it roll back down each time he reached the summit. But in Camus' version, it's a whole different ball game.

At the conclusion of *The Myth of Sisyphus*, Camus' Sisyphus rebels against the absurdity of existence by becoming—epiphanically!—fully conscious of his punishment as he reaches the summit of the hill and embracing this absurdity by accepting, joyfully, the struggle against ostensible defeat. The spectacularly surprising and perspicacious ending of Camus' essay says it all and expresses perfectly this oxymoronic contradiction of the joyful revolt against absurdity: *Il faut imaginer Sisyphe heureux* ("We must imagine Sisyphus happy").

TWENTY-THREE. Ralph and Sisyphus

For Camus, conquering the absurd, as Sisyphus in his version of the story does, consists of making sense of and understanding a world that is unreasonable and that provides no answers. It is the struggle that is required of this undertaking that counts, as Camus explains in the sentence preceding "One must imagine Sisyphus happy": "The struggle itself toward the heights is enough to fill a man's heart." So, paradoxically, for Sisyphus, happiness resides in the carrying out of the task (his punishment), not in its meaning (which goes unanswered).

But how, one might ask, is this germane to the situation—the crime and punishment—of one Ralph Theodore Joseph Branca?

First, let's discuss his "shoulder boulder" situation and how it relates to Sisyphus'. Branca's initial reaction—similar to Job's—was "Woe is me!" Consequently, during much of his adult lifetime, he continued—despite attempts (befriending Bobby Thomson, refusing to express his true feelings to the press, etc.) to rid himself of the weight of his guilt and remorse he heaped upon himself after throwing "that goddamn pitch"—to regret the consequences of that single consequential toss. (We have seen previously that Job's initial reaction to his punishment by God was an eerily similar "God damn the day I was born.") This stage was followed by his anger directed toward the Giants cheating scandal, which became a pretext for dismissing the responsibility for his own act. As opposed to Sisyphus' moment of epiphany and triumph, Ralph could never reach that epiphanic moment of victory and joy: he could never overcome his deep hatred of the Giants, and of Leo Durocher. *Ever.*

We should also consider the fundamental reasons for Ralph's and Sisyphus' punishments (within vs. without) and the punishments themselves. Despite certain similarities, the two situations are radically different: the Greek king's punishment was meted out externally, by Zeus, and not from any internal self-flagellation or paranoia on Sisyphus' part. Branca's, on the other hand, was, primarily, meted out internally, the direct result of a sense of guilt and frustration and anger. And regarding the punishments themselves, both the Greek king and the Dodgers hurler were condemned to a life (and beyond) of hardship and torture, but in Ralph's case in particular, the (self-imposed) punishment dwarfed the altogether human and irreprehensible crime.

Because of the existential weight of the boulder of defeat on his shoulders at the end of the 10/3/51 game and beyond, Ralph thus became not an existential hero following Camus' recipe, but rather an

Part Four—Crimes and Punishments

existential goat. Crushed by his one defining pitch/defeat, Branca never bounced back after '51 (hampered by injuries, he went 12–12 in the next five years) and retired humbly from baseball in 1956 after short, unremarkable stints with the Tigers and Yanks. As opposed to Camus' Sisyphus, his internal torture never quite ended.

Few great thinkers—aside from Camus, and perhaps Jean-Paul Sartre—have expressed the importance of happiness coming not from the outside world, but rather from within, more pithily and more eloquently than the nineteenth-century American philosopher Ralph Waldo Emerson, in his 1841 essay titled "Self-Reliance": "Nothing can bring you peace but yourself."

This lovely aphorism, which epitomizes Emerson's personal solution to the existential dilemma, appears at the end of the penultimate chapter (#80) of my 1997 book, *The Tao of Sports*, which was modeled structurally after Lao-Tzu's ancient text, *Tao Te Ching*:

Contentment

Are you happy with who you are? Do you look outside for approval?

Are your wishes to excel, to grow, and to improve stronger than your thoughts of victory, superiority, and control? The athlete who's happy with himself can be content with whatever the Game has to offer: adversity, rewards, surprise, even winning and losing. He can accept results not with disappointment and ecstasy, but with calm and gratitude. He can view the efforts of his opponent not with scorn, but with compassion. If he's happy with himself, he'll be content with outside events, however glorious or dismal they may appear: he has found the center. He can stand back and look at the bouncing ball with equanimity, even amusement: he's at home with the Game. Emerson was in agreement: *Nothing can bring you peace but yourself.*

If only at some point after he delivered that "goddamn pitch" to Bobby Thomson this Ralph had read that other Ralph! As a decent human being and a good and devout Catholic, Ralph Branca did indeed make frequent attempts to try to forget, to be forgiving (and even to cultivate a friendship with his nemesis, Bobby Thomson), to accept total peace within himself. But he could never truly get over it and remained "haunted" (his words) until the very end of his life with that boulder of Sisyphean regret and remorse firmly attached to his shoulders. Which is why the comparison with Camus' Sisyphus is so fascinating: Branca, and not Camus' version of Sisyphus, became the "tragic figure" of the two.

TWENTY-THREE. Ralph and Sisyphus

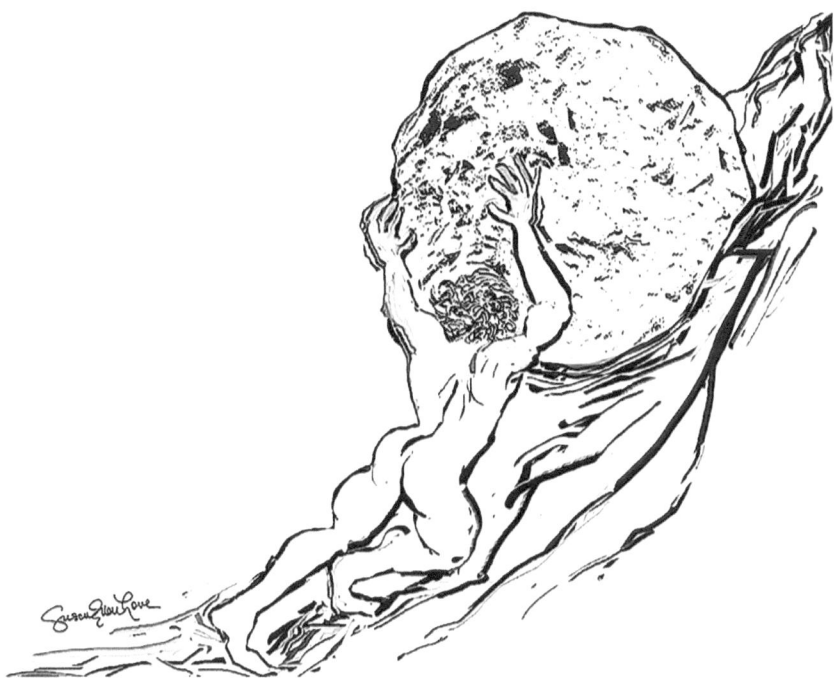

"Sisyphus Punished," by Susan Ellen Love.

From the introduction to *A Moment in Time*, here's Ralph's personal description of his tragic, lifelong plight:

> The drama of disappointment and resentment is central to this narrative. At some point, reason and rage clashed head-on.

And again, from the very end of his book:

> The better part of me wants to forgive the Giants and their scheme. Forgiving them is the right thing to do. I'm trying, but it looks like it's going to take me a couple of more years to get there.

Sadly, he never "got there." Ralph Branca died in 2016, five years after *A Moment in Time* was published. To the bitter end, he never truly forgave the Giants and Durocher, never believed that Thomson was telling the truth about seeing the fastball sign, and (despite the fact that he did generally live a full, rich, and loving life, as he says on the final page of his memoir: "The darkness of that day—October 3, 1951—has been overwhelmed by a life filled with light") passed away with that boulder

Part Four—Crimes and Punishments

of regret and sadness still attached to his weary shoulders. Were Albert Camus alive then (he died in 1960), he might have offered the following judgment as an appropriate existential Branchian obituary: *Il faut imaginer Branca malheureux.*

Despite his "life filled with light," Ralph Branca never experienced the moment of epiphanic illumination that Sisyphus reached. About which Camus might have said, in philosophical terms, that we must imagine Ralph unhappy.

Epilogue
Jean-Jacques: The Final Word

Nature made me happy and good, and if I am otherwise, it is society's fault.—Jean-Jacques Rousseau, *Emile, or On Education*

The eighteenth-century Swiss-born philosopher Jean-Jacques Rousseau, of all people, gets the final word. At the heart of his Weltanschauung (in *The Social Contract, Confessions, Emile*, and other writings) was the theory that human beings are born good and have the right to govern themselves, and that they are only corrupted by society.

Consistent with Rousseau's thinking, Ralph Theodore Joseph Branca was a human being who was born good. And he did a pretty good job governing himself, until, that is, on that gray Wednesday afternoon of October 3, 1951, at precisely 3:58 p.m. Eastern time.

But what is intriguing about the application of Rousseau's thinking to Branca's personal history is the part about the corruption of good people by the society in which they live and function. In Ralph's case, and in the cases of many of the seven literary characters just compared to it, the corrosive relationship with society played an important role in their lives.

Man/woman and society, us and others, what goes on inside and outside ourselves, the relationship between society and individuals, the existence of injustice in the world: all these issues—reflecting the Rousseauean "society corrupts" theory—occur *when good people go out into the world* and have to deal with the pressures and presence of the general populace.

Adam (the first "perfect" man, zoologist, and horticulturist), after his expulsion from Eden, proceeded to suffer out there in the world, as part of his punishment by God. Job (perfect and upright, righteous,

Epilogue

pious) had his entire world destroyed by God, but his three "friends" were not much help to him in terms of their flawed assumptions and hurtful advice for, and responses to, his impassioned speeches. For Oedipus (of noble birth, a good leader, saved Thebes from its curse), well, we know how his intercourse with the outside world ended for him. Hester (resilient, strong, kind) was unceremoniously shunned and ostracized for her sin by her community. Raskolnikov (introspective, showed signs of compassion and generosity, expressed some regret, began the road to redemption) was punished, justly, by the law and the powers that be for his murderous act and alienated from society. Josef (an innocent man) faced the cruelty and mystery of injustice showered upon him by a faceless legal system to which he was subjected. Sisyphus (an otherwise sage—his name could well have derived from *sophos*, the Greek word for "wise"—and prudent man and a king) had dealings with others (seducer, murderer, betrayer of Zeus) that resulted in his eternal torture.

And Ralph Branca (a good and decent man and a devout Catholic) was persistently haunted by the judgments that society—the press, and especially the fans—imposed upon him, as illustrated most clearly in these quotes from two consecutive pages in the introduction to his memoir (my italics in all quotes):

> *To be called* a goat—as I was—for more than half a century hurt like hell.
> *No one could forget* what had happened that afternoon in the Polo Grounds—not me, *not the country, not history itself.*
> *It pains me to be remembered* for one unfortunate pitch....

Or, as Rousseau opined in *Emile*, "Nature made me happy and good, and if I am otherwise, it is society's fault."

Actually, I lied. That great eighteenth-century thinker Jean-Jacques Rousseau doesn't actually get the last word here; this honor goes to that great twentieth-century thinker Red Smith (how fitting to circle back and have his baseball wisdom bookend this book!) and his thoughtful, eloquent quote that he bequeathed to us the day after Ralph Theodore Joseph Branca tossed that fateful, historic fastball and Robert Brown Thomson tomahawked it into the lower left-field Polo Grounds stands: "Now it is done. Now the story ends. And there is no way to tell it."

Ah, but—with all due and considerable respect—there *is* a way to tell it, Red. And I hope that in the preceding pages, I have at least made that attempt to tell the story of one epic baseball game and one historic

Epilogue

baseball pitch and one good human but flawed pitcher. And to show how this story encapsulates, in so many ways, the very ups and downs and vicissitudes of the human condition. And how this story is actually a metaphor for life—all our lives—which makes it a universal and meaningful one. It is a story with, as with all good stories, a beginning (the profound effects that one game had on so many people), a middle (the essential role losing plays in American life, and the universally human side of one American who suffered from losing), and an end (all those comparable literary crimes and punishments). All of which issues, collectively, represent an unforgettable story the meaning of which has been told many times yet is still being told, in this and doubtless in future books.

To paraphrase (but cavil) the great Red Smith: Now this book is done. Now this story ends. And there *is* indeed a way to tell it. And this book should, in fact and therefore, deserve a title that has gravitas and is large and all-encompassing and grand and human and metaphorical and that links one ballplayer from the past with the endless, universal mysteries of the human condition. And this title should probably be something like...

Ralph Branca and the Meaning of Life.

Bibliography

Aristotle. *Poetics*, in *Introduction to Aristotle*, ed. Richard McKeon. New York: The Modern Library, 1947.
Auden, W.H. *Collected Poems*, ed. Edward Mendelson. New York: Vintage, 1991.
Beckett, Samuel. *Worstward Ho*. New York: Grove, 1983.
Biegel, Brian. *Miracle Ball*. New York: Crown, 2009.
The Book of Job, trans. Stephen Mitchell. San Francisco: North Point Press, 1987.
Bradley, Bill. *Life on the Run*. New York: Bantam, 1986.
Branca, Ralph (with David Ritz). *A Moment in Time*. New York: Scribner's, 2011.
Camus, Albert. *Le Mythe de Sisyphe*. Paris: Gallimard (Collection "Idées"), 1942.
Carroll, Lewis. *Alice's Adventures in Wonderland & Through the Looking-Glass*. New York: The New American Library (Signet Classics), 1960.
Cicero. *De republica (On the Republic), De Legibus (On the Laws)*, trans. Clinton W. Keyes. Cambridge: Harvard University Press, 1928.
Confucius. *The Analects*, trans. D.C. Lau. New York: Penguin, 1998.
Dante Alighieri. *The Inferno*. London: J.M. Dent, 1962.
DeLillo, Don. *Pafko at the Wall*. New York: Scribner's, 2001.
DeLillo, Don. *Underworld*. New York: Scribner's, 1997.
Dickinson, Emily. *The Complete Poems*, ed. Thomas H. Johnson. Boston: Little, Brown, 1960.
Dostoevsky, Fyodor. *Crime and Punishment*, trans. Constance Garnett. New York: The Modern Library, 1950.
Emerson, Ralph Waldo. *Selections*, ed. Stephen E. Whicher. Cambridge, MA: Riverside, 1960.
Gay, Jason. "Willie Mays Comes Home." *GQ* (February 1, 2010).
Gilbert, W.S., and Arthur Sullivan. *The Complete Annotated Gilbert & Sullivan*, ed. Ian Bradley. New York: Oxford University Press, 1996.
Golenbock, Peter. *Bums*. New York: G.P. Putnam's, 1984.
Graham, Frank. *The New York Giants: An Informal History of a Great Baseball Club*. Carbondale: Southern Illinois University Press, 2002.
Hawthorne, Nathaniel. *The Scarlet Letter*, ed. Harry Levin. Cambridge, MA: Riverside, 1960.
Henry, O. [William Sydney Porter]. *The Best Stories of O. Henry*. New York: Doubleday, 1945.
Kafka, Franz. *The Trial*, trans. Willa and Edwin Muir. New York: The Modern Library, 1937.
Kiernan, Thomas. *The Miracle at Coogan's Bluff*. New York: Thomas Y. Crowell, 1975.
Kipling, Rudyard. *Kipling: Poems*, ed. Peter Washington. London: Everyman's Library, 2007.
Kuenster, John. *Heartbreakers: Baseball's Most Agonizing Defeats*. Chicago: Ivan R. Dee, 2001.
Lao-tzu. *Tao Te Ching*, trans. Stephen Mitchell. New York: Harper & Row, 1988.

Bibliography

Marzano, Rudy. *New York Baseball in 1951: The Dodgers, the Giants, the Yankees and the Telescope*. Jefferson, NC: McFarland, 2011.
Miller, Arthur. *The Penguin Arthur Miller: Collected Plays*. New York: Penguin, 2015.
Mitchell, Bob. *The Heart Has Its Reasons*. South Bend, IN: Diamond Communications, 1995.
Mitchell, Bob. *Once Upon a Fastball*. New York: Kensington, 2008.
Mitchell, Bob. *The Tao of Sports*. Berkeley, CA: Frog, Ltd., 1997.
Mitchell, Bob. *Time for a Heart-to-Heart*. New York: Skyhorse, 2017.
Montaigne, Michel de. *Essais*, ed. Maurice Rat. Paris: Garnier Frères, 1962.
Nolan, Bill. *The Team Time Won't Forget: The 1951 New York Giants*. Phoenix: SABR Digital Library, 2015.
The Oxford Annotated Bible, ed. Herbert G. May and Bruce M. Metzger. New York: Oxford University Press, 1962.
Pascal, Blaise. *Oeuvres complètes*, ed. Jacques Chevalier. Paris: Gallimard (Bibliothèque de la Pléiade), 1962.
Plato. *Phaedo*, in *The Works of Plato*, ed. Irwin Edman. New York: The Modern Library, 1956.
Prager, Joshua. *The Echoing Green*. New York: Pantheon, 2006.
Prager, Joshua. "Was the Giants' '51 Comeback a Miracle or Did They Simply Steal the Pennant?" *Wall Street Journal* (January 31, 2001).
Robinson, Ray. *The Home Run Heard 'Round the World*. New York: HarperCollins, 1991.
Rosten, Leo. *The New Joys of Yiddish*. New York: Crown, 2001.
Rousseau, Jean-Jacques. *Oeuvres complètes*, eds. Bernard Gagnebin et Marcel Raymond. Paris: Gallimard (Bibliothèque de la Pléiade), 2013.
Shakespeare, William. *The Complete Works*, ed. G.B. Harrison. New York: Harcourt, Brace & World, 1948.
Silverstein, Shel. *Falling Up*. New York: HarperCollins, 1996.
Smith, Red. "Miracle of Coogan's Bluff." *New York Herald Tribune* (Oct. 4, 1951).
Sophocles. *The Oedipus Plays*, trans. Paul Roche. New York: Penguin (Mentor Books), 1991.
Thomson, Bobby (with Lee Heiman and Bill Gutman). *"The Giants Win the Pennant! The Giants Win the Pennant!"* New York: Kensington, 1991.

Index

Abraham 139
Abrams, Cal 31
Adam 5, 131, 133–39, 152, 155, 159, 161, 164–65, 171
Adirondack bat 25
Aeschylus 58, 85–86
Aesop 116
Afghanistan War 73
Agamemnon 85
Ahab 116
Aldrin, Buzz 101
Alger, Horatio 48
Ali, Muhammad 47
Alice's Adventures in Wonderland 135
Allen, George 49, 61, 72
Alou, Moisés 127
An die Freude (Schiller) 152
Anagnorisis 147
The Analects 84
Antigone (character) 148
Antigone (play) 147–48
Apologie de Raimond Sebond 115
"Argument Against the Existence of a Supreme Being" 99
Aristotle 5, 85–86, 90–91, 131, 145–49
Armstrong, Lance 64
Armstrong, Neil 101
As You Like It 2
Ashburn, Richie 13, 14, 16
Associated Press 52
Atkins, Chet 66
Auden, W.H. 45, 67–68, 90
Azazel (scapegoat) 126

Bailey, George 89–90, 125
Ballesteros, Seve 50
Bamberger, George 18
Barber, Red 62
The Bard of Avon 2, 93, 134

Barkley, Charles 115–16
Barrow, Ed 104
Bartman, Steve 57, 127
Bates College 76
Baumann, Charlie 49
Bayer (aspirin) 119–20
Beatty, Warren 73
"Because of You" 123
Becker, Boris 45, 52, 60–61
Beckett, Samuel 65–66, 69
Beerbohm, Max 72
Beethoven 152
Belt Parkway 86
Bennett, Tony 123
Berger, Kati 133, 145
Berle, Milton ("Uncle Miltie") 10
Berra, Yogi 26
Best Foot Forward 73
Bible (New King James Version) 47
Bildad 141
Blake, William 143
Blane, Ralph 73
Book of Job 139
"Books of Wisdom" 139
Borough Park 7, 19
Boston College (BC) 76
Boudreau, Lou 11
Bovary, Emma 116
Bowman baseball cards 14, 18
Bradley, Bill 61
Branca, John 112, 142, 145
Branca, Mary 104
Branca, Patti 104
Branca, Raffaela 112
Brancacci Chapel 135–36, 138
Brett, George 51, 58
Brewer, Teresa 10
Brod, Max 162
Bronx Bombers 103

Index

Brooklyn, NY 7, 18–19, 28, 100, 107
Brown, Jim 58, 115
Browning, Elizabeth Barrett 2
Bruegel the Elder, Pieter 67–69
Bryant, Kobe 58
"Buckle Down, Winsocki" 74
Buckner, Bill 57, 91, 97, 112, 127
Butkus, Dick 58, 62
Butler, Rhett 69
BWAA 123

Cacciata dei progenitori dall'Eden 135–36
Caesar, Julius 93, 134
Caine, Michael 64
California Angels 127
The Call of the Wild 70
Campanella, Roy 13, 31, 40, 117
Camus, Albert 5, 131, 166–68, 170
Canio 123–25
Capra, Frank 89
Carlin, George 99
Carolina Courage 52
Carroll, Lewis 135
Caruso, Enrico 124
Catharsis 147–49
Catholic University 76
Central Connecticut State University 76
Cervantes, Miguel de 158
Chadwick, Abraham 36
Chappaqua, New York 116
Charles, Lorenzo 97
Cheney, Dick 100
Chesterfield cigarettes 22
Chesterfield label 153
Chicago Cubs 2, 40, 127
Chillingsworth, Roger 152, 154
Cicero 80, 134
Clarence (the angel) 89–90
Clemson University 49, 76
Cobb, Ty 116
Code of Hammurabi 134
Coelho, Paulo 84
Collins English Dictionary 94
Colonus 147
Como, Perry 10
Confessions 171
Confucianism 84
Confucius 84, 115
Conlan, Jocko 13
Connors, Jimmy 58–59, 116
Cooper, Chuck 116

Cooper, Mort 103
Cooper, Walker 40
Cooperstown 18
Corinth 149
Correa, Carlos 98–99
Cosette 120
Cox, Billy 24, 130
Crime and Punishment 131, 158
"Curse of the Billy Goat" 127

Daedalus 67
The Daily Telegraph 50
Dante Alighieri 45, 79, 82
Dark, Alvin 3, 14, 15, 23–24, 26, 30, 80, 105, 127
Davis, Mark 103
Day, Doris 26
De Legibus 134
Death of a Salesman 89–90, 92, 164
Decker, Mary 72
Deedes, W.F. 50
DeLillo, Don 26
Delphic Oracle (Pythia) 85, 118
Dem Bums 2, 22, 80, 98, 103, 154
Denkinger, Don 127
Deus ex machina 128
Devil Dogs 13, 16
Dickens, Charles 158
Dickinson, Emily 67, 80, 83
Dike (Fate) 148
Dimmesdale, Arthur 151–52, 155–57
La Divina Commedia 79
Djokovic, Novak 58
Doby, Larry 101–2
Doctor Faustus 116
Donatelli, Augie 13
Doohan, Peter 60
Dortmunder Union (beer) 61
Dostoevsky, Fyodor 5, 80, 131, 158–59, 166
Douglas, James "Buster" 99
Doyle Dane Bernbach 119
Drake Bakeries 13
Dressen, Chuck 24, 43, 55, 105, 127–28
Dumont TV 4, 22, 24, 26–27, 29, 53, 137
Durocher, Leo 26, 30, 36, 50, 53, 146, 167, 169

Ebbets Field 43, 53, 102, 105
Ecclesiastes 47, 139
The Echoing Green 35–37, 39
Edberg, Stefan 60

178

Index

Edison, Thomas 101
Eisenhower, Dwight (Ike) 10
Eliphaz 141
Ellerbee, Linda 14
Elpis (Hope) 80–81
Els, Ernie 61
Emerson, Ralph Waldo 85, 89, 111, 168
Emile, or On Education 171–72
Emmanuel, Tommy 66
Ennis, Del 13–14
Ephyra 166
Erskine, Carl ("Oisk") 3, 53, 55, 105, 128
Essais 115
Eteocles 147
Eve 133–37
Evert, Chris 47
Everyman 5, 87, 89–93, 104, 135
Exodus 134

Falling Up 111
Farewell Address (Lou Gehrig) 103–4
Favre, Brett 58
Fear Strikes Out 73
Felton, Happy 31
Field of Dreams, 105
Fisher, Eddie 10
Fisk, Carlton 97
Fitzgerald, F. Scott 116
Flatbush 10
Flaubert, Gustave 116, 158
Florida Marlins 127
Flutie, Doug 97
Ford, Ernie 10
Fortuna (Roman goddess of luck) 106–7
Foster's (beer) 52
Frankenstein, Victor 116
Franklin, Benjamin 112
Franks, Herman 36
Frazier, Joe 47
Furillo, Carl 13

Gable, Dan 63
Gandhi, Mahatma 114
Garcia, Sergio 50
Garden of Eden 134–37, 155, 171
Garnett, Kevin 116
Gatsby, Jay 116
Gay, Jason 40
Gehrig, Lou 99, 103–4
Genesis 133–34
Georgia Tech 76
Gerulaitis, Vitas 116

The Giants Win the Pennant! The Giants Win the Pennant! 58, 93
Gibson, Bob 58
Gilbert, W.S. 98, 134, 165
GOAT 3, 90, 128–30
Goldberg, Rube 36
Gonzalez, Alex 91
Gonzalez, Pancho 58
Gooden, Dwight 111
GQ magazine 40
Grand Central Station 116
Gray, Elisha 101
Gray, Ted 141, 161
Greenwald, Hank 97
Grissom, Marv 13
Grosjean, Sebastien 62

Hackl, Georg 61
Hades 79
Halloween 2
Hamartia 90, 145–46
Hamlet (character) 55
Hamm, Mia 52
Hamner, Granny 14
Harris, Franco 97
Hartung, Clint 3, 15, 24, 53
Harwell, Ernie 14, 16, 18, 25, 137
"The Hawk" 149
Hawthorne, Nathaniel 5, 131, 151, 153
Hayes, Woody 49, 72–73, 116
Hearn, Jim 53
The Heart Has Its Reasons 48
Henri, O. 80
Hingle, Pat 73
Hirschberg, Lynn 64
Hodges, Gil 13, 24, 55, 105, 127
Hodges, Russ 153, 157
Hogan, Ben 47, 58
Holden, William 15
Holtz, Lou 50
Hoover, Herbert 71
Howe, Gordie 58
Huggins, Miller 104
Hugo, Victor 120, 163

I May Be Wrong But I Doubt It 115–16
Iago 34
Icarus 67, 69, 116
Illustrations of the Book of Job 143
Indiana University 49, 76
Inferno 79, 82
Iolanthe 165

Index

Iowa State University 76
Iraq War 73
Irvin, Monte 3, 15–16, 24, 26, 80
Isaac 139
It's a Wonderful Life 89
Ivanovna, Alyona 158

Jablonski, Ray 13
Jacksonville University 76
Jacobs, Joe 35
Jansen, Larry 81
Janus (Roman God) 110, 121–23
Japanese internment camps 126
Jefferson, Thomas 95
Jesus Christ 114–15
Jim Crow laws 126
Job 5, 131, 139–44, 152, 159, 164–65, 167, 171
Jocasta 145, 147
Joel, Billy 140
Johns Hopkins University 75
Johnson, Rafer 72
Jones, Deacon 62
Jones, Willie "Puddin' Head" 13
Jorda, Lou 117
Jordan, Michael 58
Joyce, James 158
Joyner-Kersee, Jackie 58
Julius Caesar 93

K., Josef 5, 131, 162–65, 172
Kafka, Franz 5, 131, 162–64, 166
Keiter, Les 12
Kelly, Gene 73
Kennedy, John F. 57
Kennedy, Robert F. 95
King, Billie Jean 58
King, Larry 5, 7, 28–34, 62
King, Martin Luther, Jr. 95
King of Thebes 145, 147
Kinsella, Ray 105
Kipling, Rudyard 45, 47–48, 52–53, 55
Knight, Bobby 49, 116
Knopfler, Mark 66
Konikowski, Alex 31
Korean War 10, 73
Koslo, Dave 31
Kottke, Leo 66
Koufax, Sandy 30
Kramer, Jack 31
Krumholz, Michael 100–1
Kukla, Fran, and Ollie 11

Labine, Clem 53, 128
Laettner, Christian 97
Laius 145–48
Landry, Tom 49
Landscape with the Fall of Icarus (painting) 67
"Landscape with the Fall of Icarus" (poem) 68
Lao-tzu 38, 47, 84–85, 168
Larry King Now 7, 29
"The Last Leaf" 80
The Last Supper 103
Lennon, John 157
Leonard, Justin 72
Leoncavallo, Ruggiero 123
Levet, Thomas 52, 61
Leviticus 126, 134
Lewis, Lennox 116
Lewis, Tommy 116
Lex talionus 134, 152
Lieberman, Nancy 58
The Little Engine That Could 48
Lockman, Whitey 3, 14–16, 24, 26, 53, 127, 130
Lollabrigida, Gina 51
Loman, Linda 90, 164
Loman, Willy 90–92, 164–65
Lombardi, Ernie 127
Lombardi, Vince 49, 72–73
London, Jack 70
Lopez, Nancy 58
The Lord Chancellor 165
Louis, Joe 73
Louisiana State University 23, 30
Love, Susan Ellen 29, 32–33, 65, 169

Macbeth (character) 1
Macbeth (play) 3, 128
Mack, Connie 117
Maeterlinck, Maurice 95
Maglie, Sal 14, 30, 41
Malden, Karl 73
Mandela, Nelson 114
Manichaean 24
Mantle, Mickey 98–99
Marciano, Rocky 73
Marcus Aurelius 85
Marlowe, Christopher 116
Marmeladov, Sonya 158–59
Marquette University 75–76
Marshall, Willard 40
Martin, Dean 10

Index

Martin, Hugh 73
Masaccio 135–38
Mathews, Eddie 5
Mathewson, Christy 111
Mays, Willie 16, 26, 30, 40, 43, 53, 81, 98–99, 105, 117, 129
McCarthy, Joe (baseball manager) 104
McCarthyism 126
McCovey, Willie 97
McEnroe, John 116
McNeese State University 76
Medea 19
Melville, Herman 116, 158
Menander 85
The Merchant of Venice 34
Merkle, Fred 91, 127
Merope 149
Merriam-Webster's 94
The Metamorphosis 165
Mighty Mouse 53
The Mikado 98, 134
Miller, Arthur 89–92
Milwaukee Braves 5
Minneapolis Millers 154
Miracle at Coogan's Bluff 1, 7, 15, 29, 127, 157, 159
Les Misérables 119, 163
Moegle, Dickie 116
A Moment in Time 4, 37, 82, 87, 93, 102, 122, 125, 147, 169
Montaigne, Michel de 114–15, 118
Moore, Donnie 57, 127
Mother Teresa 114
Mueller, Don 3, 15, 24, 55, 80, 105, 127–28
Mulvey, Ann 104, 125, 147
Murray, Andy 58
"Musée des Beaux-Arts" 67, 90
Musial, Stan 13, 14, 47
Le Mythe de Sisyphe 131, 166

Nadal, Rafa 58
Narcissus 116
Navratilova, Martina 47, 58
NCAA 47, 72, 97
Nedda 123
New York Mets 5
New York Times 10, 18, 39, 64, 144
New York University (NYU) 77–78
New York Yankees 30, 47
Newcombe, Don 3, 23–24, 55, 80–81, 105, 127–28

Newton, Sir Isaac 110, 113
Nicklaus, Jack 47, 58
Nietzsche, Friedrich 99
"The Nightmare Song" 165
Ninth Symphony (Beethoven) 152
Nitschke, Wolfgang 63
Noble, Ray 81
Norman, Magnus 62
North Carolina State University 80
Norworth, Jack 45, 57

"Ode to Joy" (Beethoven) 152
Oedipus 5, 116, 131, 145–49, 152, 159, 163–65, 172
Oedipus at Colonus 148
Oedipus Rex 131, 145, 147–49
Oklahoma (musical) 81
Old Testament 126, 131, 133–34, 139
Oldmasters Museum (Brussels) 69
"Ollie" (Oliver J. Dragon) 11, 14, 18
Olympic credo 52
"On Opponents" 48–49
Once Upon a Fastball 28, 37
Oregon State University 76
Ostilly, Seymon 118–20
Othello 34
Ovechkin, Alex 58
Owen, Mickey 91, 127
Owens, Jesse 58
Oxford English Dictionary (OED) 94

Pafko, Andy 13, 16, 24–26, 55, 62, 80, 98, 105, 130
Page, Patti 10
Pagliacci (opera) 123–24
Pagliaccio (character) 123
Paige, Satchel 40
Palmer, Arnold 47
Palmer Raids 126
Pandora 79, 81
Le pari (Pascal's Wager) 114
Pascal, Blaise 113–14
Pathos 147
Patton, George S. 73
Paul, Les 66
Pearl (Hester Prynne's daughter) 151, 157
Pearl Harbor 57
Pensées (Pascal) 113
Pep, Willie 118
Pepper, Dottie 58
Peripeteia 146–47

181

Index

Perkins, Tony 73
Pesky, Johnny 51
Petrovich, Porfiry 159–60
Phaedo 67
Phalen, Gerard 97
Piersall, Jimmy 73
Plato 67, 85
Pledge of Allegiance 94
Plimpton, George 39
Poetics 90, 131, 145, 149
Polo Grounds 22, 30, 38, 42, 85, 97, 102, 105, 130, 133, 140
Polybus 149
Polyneices 147
Pope, Alexander 53, 80
Portia 34
Poulter, Ian 50
Prager, Joshua 35–36, 38–39, 133, 141, 144, 155
Presley, Elvis 10
Proust, Marcel 7, 21, 158
Proverbs 139
Der Prozess 163
Prynne, Hester 5, 131, 151–57, 159, 164–65, 172
Psalms 139
Pyrrhonism 115

Queen Elizabeth 19

Ralph Branca and the Meaning of Life 173
Raskolnikov, Rodion Romanovich 5, 131, 158–60, 163–65, 172
Rawlings PM1 (baseball mitt) 11, 13, 18
Ray, Johnny 10
Red Scare 126
Reed, Neil 49
Reese, Pee Wee 153
Renard, Jules 94–95
Repulski, Eldon "Rip" 13
Revolutionary War 73
Richardson, Bobby 97
Rickey, Branch 107
Rigney, Bill 40
Ritz, David 125
Roberts, Robin 23
Robinson, Jackie 4, 13, 23, 26, 47, 58, 101–2, 105, 107, 128, 130
Robinson, Joe 66
Rockne, Knute 72
Rodman, Dennis 116

Rogers, Roy 53
Rome Summer Olympics 72
Roosevelt, Franklin Delano 57
Rose, Pete 58, 116
Rosenberg, Ethel 128
Rosenberg, Julius 128
The Rosenbergs 126
Rosten, Leo 28–29
Rousseau, Jean-Jacques 171–72
Rowley, Father Pat 4, 58, 106, 140, 158, 162
Ruppert, Jacob 104
Russell, Bill 116
Rutigliano, Sam 62
Ryder Cup 47, 50, 72

Sacco and Vanzetti 126
St. Petersburg 158
Salem witch trials 126
Samsa, Gregor 165
Sanders, Barry 115
Sartre, Jean-Paul 168
Satan 139
The Scarlet Letter 131, 151, 153, 157
Schaap, Dick 32
Schadenfreude 16, 126, 130, 152–54
Schenz, Hank 36
Schiller, Friedrich, 152
Schmeling, Max 35, 94
School of Visual Arts 118
Seaver, Tom 50
"Self-Reliance" 111, 168
Seneca the Younger 85, 107, 111
September 11, 2001 57
Serling, Rod 138
Shakespeare, William 2, 3, 34, 93–94, 128, 134
Sharkey, Jack 94
Shaw, George Bernard 7
Shelley, Mary 116
Sherman, Richard 116
Shot Heard 'Round the World 1, 15
Shuba, George "Shotgun" 31
Sianis, Billy 127
Siberia 159–60
Silverstein, Shel 111
Silvio 123
Sing Sing 128
Sisyphus 5, 131, 166–70, 172
Slaughter, Enos 13
Smart, Keith 97
Smith, Lonnie 91

182

Index

Smith, Red 1, 172
Smith-Corona (typewriter) 74
Snead, Sam 47
Snider, Duke 13, 14
Sobie Ron, 117
The Social Contract 171
Society for American Baseball Research (SABR) 2
Socrates 115
Sophocles 5, 131, 145
Spaldeen (rubber ball) 12–17, 100
Splendor in the Grass 73
Sports Illustrated 5
Sprewell, Latrell 116
Stalag 17 15
Stein, Barney 54, 136
Steinbrenner, George 62
Stewart, James 89
Stoic philosophers 85
Sugar, Bert 116–18
Sukeforth, Clyde 3, 55, 105, 127–28
Sukenik, Irv 103
Sullivan, Sir Arthur 98–99, 134, 165
Swarthmore College 76

"Take Me Out to the Ball Game" 57, 76
The Tao of Sports 51, 168
Tao Te Ching 38, 47, 84, 168
Taoism 84
Tarango, Jeff 116
Taurasi, Diana 58
Taylor, Don 15
Temple of Apollo at Delphi 85
Tennessee State University 75
Texaco Star Theater 10
Thanksgiving turkey 126
"Theban plays" 148
Thebes 147, 172
Third Law of Motion (Newton's) 110
Thompson, Hank 14, 16
Time for a Heart-to-Heart 28
Tiresias 146–47
Tittle, Y.A. 30, 72
Topps baseball cards 10, 14, 18
Torgeson, Earl 13–14
Torres, Mike 57
Tour de France 64
Tracy, Dick 53
Travis, Merle 66
Tree of the Knowledge of Good and Evil 133
The Trial 131, 162–64

TV Westerns 23, 126
Tyndale, William 126
Tyson, Mike 116

Underwood (typewriter) 74
U.S. Constitution 94, 134
University of Arkansas 76
University of California, Santa Cruz 75
University of Colorado 76
University of Florida 76
University of Georgia 76
University of Kansas 76
University of Michigan 71, 74
University of Minnesota 76
University of Nebraska–Omaha 76
University of Notre Dame 74
University of Oklahoma 75–76
University of Pennsylvania (Penn) 76
University of Rhode Island 75
University of Richmond 75
University of Tennessee 76
University of Utah 75–76
University of Vermont 76
University of West Virginia 76
University of Wisconsin 74
University of Wyoming 76

Valentine, Bobby 104
Valjean, Jean 163
Valvano, Jimmy 26, 72, 80
Van Cuyk, Chris 31
Van de Velde, Jean 52, 61
Verrazano-Narrows Bridge 86
"*Vesti la giubba*" 123
Vietnam War 73
"The Voice" 111

Waitkus, Eddie 23
Wake Forest University 76
Walker, Rube 31, 40, 55, 117
Wall Street Journal 35, 141
Washington Freedom 52
Webster, Daniel 95
Die Werwandlung 165
West, Jerry 58–59
Westchester County 133, 144
Westfield, Alabama 117
Westrum, Wes 5
White Fang 70
Wide World of Sports (ABC) 71
Wilhelm, Hoyt 13
Williams, Davey 14, 30

Index

Williams, Serena 52
Williams, Venus 52
Williams, William Carlos 68
Williams College 135
Wilson, Hack 127
Wilson, Mookie 91, 97, 112, 127
Wimbledon 47, 55, 60, 64
Winsocki Military Academy, 74
WMGM-AM 32
Wollensak (telescope) 36
Wooden, John 49, 115, 120
Woods, Ickey 116
Woolf, Virginia 158
Worcester State University 76
World War I 73
World War II 73

Worstward Ho 65
WPIX 23
WUSA 52

Yale University 47, 73–74
Yang, C.K. 72
Yankee Doodles 13, 16
Yankee Stadium 103
Yom Kippur 126, 129
Young, Cy 30
Yvars, Sal 18, 36–37, 41, 149

Zaharias, Babe 58
Zeno 55
Zeus 85, 166–67, 172
Zophar 141

www.ingramcontent.com/pod-product-compliance
Lightning Source LLC
Chambersburg PA
CBHW021857230426
43671CB00006B/431